HISTORY IN CAMERA

VICTORIA'S WARS

I. F. W. BECKETT

Shire Publications Ltd

£1·90

Published in 1998 by Shire Publications Ltd, Cromwell House, Church Street, Princes Risborough, Buckinghamshire HP27 9AA, UK.
Copyright © 1974 by I. F. W. Beckett. First published 1974; reprinted 1987. Second edition 1998. Number 2 in the History in Camera series. ISBN 0 7478 0388 9.
I. F. W. Beckett is hereby identified as the author of this work in accordance with Section 77 of the Copyright, Designs and Patents Act, 1988.

British Library Cataloguing in Publication Data. A catalogue record for this book is available from the British Library.

Printed in Great Britain by CIT Printing Services Ltd, Press Buildings, Merlins Bridge, Haverfordwest, Pembrokeshire SA61 1XF.

The cover design by Ron Shaddock shows a Maxim-gun detachment of 1st Battalion King's Royal Rifle Corps, Chitral Campaign, 1895. Early machine guns had been developed in the American Civil War but the early Gatlings, Nordenfelts and Gardners were not very reliable. In 1883 Hiram Maxim developed his famous Maxim gun, firing two thousand rounds in only three minutes.

The illustration on the title page is Fenton's photograph of the cookhouse of the 8th Hussars in the Crimea.

Contents

Below: 'Silent Sue', 16th Brigade Royal Artillery's 5-inch lyddite cow-gun in action at Paul Kop, Orange River Colony, during the South African War. Shrapnel was the main ammunition for field guns but lyddite, a form of explosive invented at Lydd in Kent, was the shell fired by howitzers and heavier guns. First used at Omdurman, it had proved capable of killing men up to 50 yards from the point of impact by the shock of detonation. This cow-gun, pulled by oxen, was the military version of the naval 4.7-inch gun, which also fired a lyddite shell.

The author expresses his thanks to the staff of the Department of Records, National Army Museum, Chelsea.

The photographs in this book, except for those listed below, are reproduced by kind permission of the National Army Museum.
Other photographs are acknowledged as follows: Auckland Public Library Photography Collection, pages 34 and 36 (top and bottom); Radio Times Hulton Picture Library, pages 58 and 60.

General Roberts and staff inspecting captured guns in Kabul (Second Afghan War). Roberts, with two brigades of infantry and one of cavalry, had set out on 30th September 1879, broken through the Charasia defile on 6th October, and occupied Kabul, capturing seventy-five abandoned guns.

Introduction

The basic problem for the Victorian army was to meet its rapidly expanding commitments of home and imperial defence in the context of voluntary enlistment and a basically anti-militarist society. There was, however, a strange paradox in the attitude towards the army, for though not a specifically military nation the British were decidedly warlike.

Deeply rooted in the civilian attitude was the fear of a large standing army, the traditions of which stretched back to Cromwell's major generals, James II and a licentious, billeted soldiery. The army cost money, considerably more in fact than the navy which had a more obvious value to the Victorian mind. Indeed the middle classes regarded the army as largely incidental to the progress of country and Empire even though the army was the agent by which the Empire was extended and policed. Concerned only that the Empire should be financed on a shoestring, the public were indifferent to the conditions and requirements of the army, save in occasional panics which alone could stir public opinion in favour of reform. The War Office itself was not a popular ministry with politicians and several incumbents died as a result of the strain. The considerable pride taken in military achievements was not reflected in concern for the army itself.

After the Napoleonic Wars the British Army was largely allowed to stagnate in a suffocating climate of false government economy and public apathy. From a total of around 220,000 men in 1815 the army declined to 94,500 in 1841 though it recovered to 152,000 by 1854. The Duke of Wellington, Commander-in-Chief 1827-8 and 1842-52, had been forced by the emphasis on retrenchment to preserve a nucleus of fighting men at the expense of supporting services. There were the additional forces available to the East India Company, amounting to some 315,000 men and advantageously paid for by the Indian authorities, but they were not readily available for use much beyond India's

frontiers until after the Crown assumed responsibility for the Indian
army following the Mutiny in 1857.

Administration was divided between thirteen differing authorities
with ill-defined and conflicting responsibilities. Among these were
included the Commander-in-Chief, broadly responsible for command,
discipline and patronage and representative of royal authority; the Master
General of Ordnance responsible for technical supplies; the Secretary
of State for War and the Colonies responsible for the employment of
the army outside the United Kingdom; and the Secretary at War responsible for finance and the army's spokesman in the Commons. The
Treasury controlled the Commissariat departments and the Home Office administered the Militia. This did not aid the proper development
of co-ordinated planning and, as a result, most expeditions were hastily
improvised .

The army was still recruited from the lowest elements of society who
found there the food, shelter and security denied to them in civilian life.
However, the social misfits, unemployed, criminals and Irish, who
constituted the rank and file, had to be held together by a rigid discipline — indeed flogging was not abolished finally until 1881. Pay was
low and drunkenness rife, which was not surprising considering that
most service was spent in unhealthy foreign stations. Until 1847 enlistment was between twenty-one and twenty-four years, and thereafter
for twelve years, before the Cardwell reforms. The army had a growing
recruitment crisis which it was never to resolve. Yet between 1815 and
1852 the small army fought seventeen major campaigns in India, Afghanistan, Burma, Ceylon, China, South Africa, Canada and New Zealand.

The majority of officers were appointed and promoted up to lieutenant colonel's rank by purchase. This system of buying rank step by step
had originated under Charles I but was regularised by George I with an
official tariff for prices. However, actual prices were frequently far in
excess of the tariff; for example the Earl of Lucan, commander of the
Cavalry Division in the Crimean War, purchased command of the 17th
Lancers in 1826 for £25,000. The defenders of purchase claimed that
the army attracted only men of wealth and position who would not
challenge the established order as a professional officer corps might. It
was felt that purchase preserved the essential and indeed unique *esprit
de corps* of the British regimental system. In any case the alternative
did not recommend itself to the taxpayer. The officer class was not on
the whole very interested in the more professional aspects of military

life and original thinking on strategic or tactical problems was not widespread. The Peninsular legacy dogged even talented minds such as Sir Patrick MacDougall and Sir John Fox Burgoyne.

Nonetheless, younger officers did begin to demonstrate increasing professionalism with the establishment of professional bodies such as the United Service Institution in 1819 and the Royal Artillery Institution in 1840 while professional military journals began to appear in the 1820s and 1830s. Higher standards were introduced in military training and professional education including, for example, the establishment of the artillery and engineering schools at Shoeburyness and Chatham in 1852 and the musketry school at Hythe in 1853. Even the position of the ordinary private soldier underwent some transformation through the efforts of Henry Grey, Viscount Howick who as successively Secretary at War and Secretary of State for War and the Colonies in the 1830s and 1840s introduced some alternative recreations to drink in barracks and tried to improve the army's health by a system of rotation to enable regiments to become acclimatised to hotter climates before being sent to the West Indies. It was Grey who also instituted the changes in the terms of service in 1847.

However Wellington himself was a formidable obstacle to reform, resisting equally strongly the extension of either royal or political control over the army. The Commons in any case would not bear the cost of reform and all major military figures opposed change. The army feared debate in Parliament would lead to further redundancies. But demand for reform mounted with the invasion panics of the 1840s inspired by the fear that the introduction of steam ships had violated the traditional barrier of the Channel. Unfortunately, however, those reforms already begun by Wellington's successor, Lord Hardinge, had hardly begun to yield benefits and the army remained organised and trained for small wars against non-European opponents rather than the large scale continental-style challenge that faced it in the Crimea. The Crimean War (1854-6) was a considerable shock to the public. The poor staff work, breakdown in transport, supply and medical services and the appalling tactical blunders had a great impact through the reports of W. H. Russell of *The Times*. The war severely strained British resources and militia regiments had to be sent to garrison Mediterranean bases. The Indian Mutiny so stretched the available troops that only fourteen battalions were left in England in August 1857. The renewal of invasion fears in 1859 led to the formation of the Rifle Volunteers, a cheap but hardly adequate substitute for a trained reserve. The rapid victories of Prussian conscript armies in Denmark in 1864 and Austria in 1866 added to the growing recognition that reform was vital. Some things were accomplished as a result of the Crimean debacle. The posts of Master General of Ordnance and Secretary at War were abolished and the Treasury and Home Office were relieved of their share of administration. The duties were divided between the Commander-in-Chief and the Secretary of State for War, now free of the Colonial Office. Both Sidney Herbert and General Jonathan Peel as successive Secretaries of State attempted wider reforms but were not conspicuously successful.

The first major attempt to solve the problems facing the army was undertaken by Edward Cardwell (Secretary of State 1868-74). The Cardwell reforms should not, however, be seen as a beginning, but rather as a culmination, of the processes begun before the Crimean War. They were designed to continue Herbert's departmental reconstruction, to end purchase and, most important of all, to solve the recruiting problem. The solution envisaged by Cardwell was linked battalions and short service to build up a reserve. By this, service with the colours was reduced to six years with a further six years in the reserve. Regular battalions would be linked with one battalion at a home depot supplying the drafts for a partner battalion abroad. Localisation of the regulars with localities and with auxiliary forces would aid recruiting. Also colonial garrisons were withdrawn from Australia, New Zealand and Canada which were now compelled to defend themselves. Purchase was abolished, in the face of much opposition, by royal warrant and the Commander-in-Chief became the military adviser to the Secretary of State. Administration was now divided between Commander-in-Chief, Financial Secretary and Surveyor General of Ordnance. To demonstrate the subordination of the Commander-in-Chief to the Secretary of State, the Duke of Cambridge (Commander-in-Chief 1856-95) was removed from the Horse Guards to the War Office in Pall Mall.

On paper the system looked fine but Cardwell had ignored possible strains on linked battalions from small wars; he had not foreseen recruiting difficulties and he had not foreseen the drain on the home battalions. This was due to a certain extent to his ignorance of military affairs and the pressures under which he worked. Almost at once the balance of battalions was upset by the Ashanti War; in 1872 there had been seventy battalions at home and seventy-one abroad but by 1879 there were only fifty-nine at home and eighty-two abroad. There was continual strain with crises in Egypt, South Africa and Afghanistan. The correct balance was never attained and under false government economies the home battalions were reduced to 'squeezed lemons' with the reserve being utilised to replace the young and unfit soldiers in home units on the outbreak of war. Both the Stanley Committee of 1876 and Airey Committee of 1878-9 showed the defects but were ignored. In 1881 Hugh Childers completed the Cardwell scheme by permanently linking the battalions (territorialisation) and mak- ing auxiliary forces battalions of the regular regiment. This largely failed to encourage local recruiting as the bulk of recruits still came from the north and the large depots were in the south. The 'Pimlico Highlanders' thus became a popular image of the unlikely composition of some of the new county regiments.

The root of the problem was, of course, recruiting. The army's pay was distinctly uncompetitive and there was a close correlation between recruit- ing and unemployment figures – what Field Marshal Lord Nicholson later called the compulsion of destitution. The competition of labour, decline of rural population and Irish emigration all hit the army. Other unattractive features were foreign duty, insanitary barracks, harsh discipline, lack of recreation, the discouragement of marriage, the lack of training in trades and a complete lack of government provision for veterans or reservists in civilian life. For many families the ultimate disgrace was enlistment and indeed soldiers were objects of discrimination at public entertainments such as theatres and restaurants. There was no alternative but declining age limits and physical standards, though in 1881 Childers forebade youths of under twenty from serving abroad. The poor quality of short-service sol- diers was made the scapegoat for many of the disasters that befell British armies in the 1880s. Excluding a rise in pay, which was naturally unpopu- lar with the taxpayer, the only alternative was conscription but this was seen by politicians as tantamount to political suicide, even though there had been something like it during the Napoleonic Wars. In any case con- scription was by no means compatible with the need to furnish foreign drafts. The problem was virtually insoluble and was made worse by the accepted governmental economic remedy, to cut the estimates, of reducing either stores or men. At least the Indian army cost the British taxpayer nothing, for the burden of its upkeep and that of the British troops in India fell on the Indian taxpayer. The Indian army proved itself more than useful in numerous campaigns outside India, for example, Abyssinia in 1867, Malta in 1878 and Egypt and the Sudan 1882-99.

It might be supposed that abolition of purchase changed the structure of the officer corps, but it changed little, the pre-1870 seniority still prevail- ing. The classes from which the officers were drawn did not alter conspicu- ously down to 1914 and the low financial rewards, high cost of living and regimental tradition went far to ensure the continuing predominance of the public schools. Unfortunately the schools did not teach military subjects and the army, except in its technical branches, tended to receive the less intellectually able products of the public schools. Opportunities to study were not widespread and the Staff College established in 1858 had a hard struggle for acceptance. Paradoxically one of the most celebrated soldiers of the Victorian army advanced without benefit of money.

Garnet Wolseley (1833-1913) gained his first commission by virtue of his father's service and advanced by merit through action in Burma, the Crimea and China. His first independent command was the 1870 Red River Expedition in Canada. In 1873 he commanded in the Ashanti War and this was followed by administrative service in Cyprus and South Africa. By the 1880s Wolseley had become universally known as 'Our Only General' and the model for Gilbert and Sullivan's 'modern major-general'. The height of his success was the annexation of Egypt in 1882 although his active military career ended with the failure to save Gordon in Khartoum in 1885. Wolseley thereafter followed his period as Adjutant General as Commander-in-Chief, Ireland, and finally as Commander-in-Chief (1895-1900) though by this time his faculties were rapidly failing. His successor as Commander-in-Chief was his rival Lord Roberts.

Roberts (1832-1914) entered the Bengal Artillery as a second lieutenant in 1851 and won the Victoria Cross in the Mutiny. His reputation was made as Commander of the Afghan Field Force on the march from Kabul to relieve Kandahar in the Second Afghan War. Roberts rose to be Commander-in-Chief, India, 1885-93, to Commander-in-Chief, Ireland, 1895-9 and was sent to command in South Africa in 1899. He succeeded Wolseley as Commander-in-Chief, and was the last incumbent of this office which was abolished in 1904. After campaigning unsuccessfully for compulsory service, Roberts died on a visit to the Indian Contingent in France in 1914.

The Victorian army had obvious duties in home defence, imperial garrisons and small wars, yet there was no clear definition of its actual purpose and function and no real plan for imperial defence. Much of the problem lay in the continuing confused administrative set-up of the War Office where power was divided between civilians and the military. The administrative reforms of the period after 1870 should be seen in the light of a continuing struggle between the two groups, notably over the means by which the civilians controlled the army – finance. Knowing full well the Treasury attitude, the army always demanded too much in order to compensate for normal reductions. In the words of one royal commission: 'extravagance controlled by stinginess is not likely to result either in economy or efficiency.' The army never fully understood that their advice had to be related to the party political and economic pressures on the Cabinet. The army was not in fact technically responsible for its advice and there was always a problem of translating professional knowledge to civilians who did not understand it. Apart from this internal civil-military struggle, the army was also plagued by the rival 'rings' of Roberts and Wolseley competing for the choice of appointments on staffs and expeditions; by the continual struggle with the Treasury; and with the Crown, in the person of the Duke of Cambridge, trying to exert influence.

Yet, despite the tremendous problems with recruitment and administration, the Victorian army excelled in its 'small wars'. There was hardly a year without a campaign somewhere in the Empire for annexation, to guarantee frontiers, to restore order or to punish those who violated *Pax Britannica*. In such campaigns the army fought not only the enemy but usually terrain, climate and topographical ignorance as well. Transport and supply had to be largely improvised and often time was limited due to risks of disease or climatic changes. The opponents were colourful and varied, ranging from Afghans to Zulus, Maoris, Dervishes and Boers. The enemy had the advantage of local knowledge and were often formidable foes in their own element, which offset the British advantage in fire power. The absence of a staff caused Wolseley to utilise the most talented men available but this 'ring' bred resentment of favouritism and did not in fact encourage initiative in its members. The campaigns gave the Victorian army great practical opportunities to learn military methods and improvisation but the tactical lessons were few due to the retention of obsolete squares and volleys suitable for fighting primitive peoples but not Europeans. At least the campaigns did lead to a more comfortable campaign dress and the gradual introduction of khaki. In 1896 C. E. Callwell published *Small Wars: Their Principles and Practice* designed as the official War Office text on colonial campaigns.

In terms of proper planning the obvious remedy was a general staff on the European pattern, but this was unacceptable to the politicians, especially the Liberals. A Topographical and Statistical Branch had been formed in 1855 but this was largely dormant until revived as the Intelligence Department by Wolseley in 1886 and placed under the supervision of the energetic Henry Brackenbury. The 1889 Hartington Commission reported in 1891 that the Commander-in-Chief should be abolished and a War Office Council and General Staff set up to give the Secretary the best possible military advice. The proposals were rejected although an Army Board and Joint Naval and Military Committee was set up. But British military planning was still dominated by the fear of invasion and by the fears of a Russian attack on India. In 1888 Edward Stanhope in his celebrated memorandum for the first time attempted to list the army's priorities – support for the civil power in the United Kingdom, the defence of India, imperial garrisons, home defence and an army for foreign service. A European involvement was regarded as sufficiently improbable to make any preparations unnecessary. A Standing Defence Committee of the Cabinet was established in 1895 and in the same year the Duke of Cambridge was finally retired, the opportunity being taken to reduce the powers of the commander-in-chief in relation to those of the Secretary of State, which only increased the friction between the new incumbent, Wolseley, and the government. It is perhaps surprising in view of the close co-operation of the navy on many colonial expeditions that there was no real joint planning before the First World War.

The Boer War (1899-1902) was a severe shock to the country. It was almost as if there had been no progress at all since 1854. But the war generated much-needed drastic reforms to fit the army for a European or Indian conflict. Successive Secretaries of State, St John Brodrick (1901-3), H. O. Arnold-Forster (1903-5) and the Liberal R. B. Haldane (1905-12) prepared the British army well. In 1914 the small BEF was arguably the best fighting force ever to leave the shores of Britain, but ultimately in 1916 the country had to resort to the solution shunned by the Victorians – conscription, for the army still reflected the long-standing failure to match resources to commitments.

This selection of photographs, many never previously published, shows the Victorian soldier in a variety of climes and conditions, from Burma in 1852 to the last great imperial adventure in Tibet in 1903-4. Genuine action photographs were, of course, impossible due to the primitive nature of the photographic equipment but this does not detract from the interest nor indeed from the quality of some of the earliest examples.

The British Empire was largely built on shifting strategic sands and it was, as Disraeli well knew, the belief of the British in themselves that maintained it amidst the envy and hate of lesser powers. The Empire has gone, destroyed as much from within as without, but the memory of that great adventure remains a monument to the endeavour and achievement of that oft neglected Victorian army.

Second Burma War, 1852-3

The dynasty that ruled Burma from the court of Ava, 'the Centre of the Universe', became a threat to British India in 1818 when the Burmese king laid claim to the provinces of East Bengal. The East India Company was forced to fight in 1823 when the Burmese actually invaded Bengal. The British force under Major General Sir A. Campbell occupied Rangoon in 1824 at a cost of fifteen thousand dead, mainly from disease. By the Treaty of Yandabu Britain annexed Assam, Arakan and Tennasserim.

Relations with the unstable kings of Burma declined and the British resident was withdrawn from Ava in 1840. English merchants were advised not to visit Burma but by 1852 the Burmese governor of Rangoon was becoming notorious for his extortion from British subjects. The Governor General of India, the Marquis of Dalhousie, sent a squadron under Commodore Lambert to prevent further ill-treatment. Dalhousie, who could see no particular advantage in a war, was finally forced to send an ultimatum. This was ignored and the Second Burma War had begun.

In a model campaign Major General Godwin, with only 5,700 men including the 18th, 51st and 80th Foot, seized Mantaban on 5th April 1852 and stormed Rangoon on 11th to 14th April against a reputed Burmese garrison of 10,000 men. On 4th June Commander Tarleton of HMS *Fox* and his small Irrawaddy flotilla took Pegu, in revolt against the Burmese kings, and on 9th July 1852 Tarleton briefly occupied Prome. Dalhousie decided to annex Pegu (Lower Burma) and Godwin reoccupied Prome on 10th October and Pegu on 21st November. The British forces lost only 377 dead in eight months and the whole affair cost less than £2 million. Dalhousie, feeling that negotiations would be pointless, annexed Lower Burma by proclamation in December 1852. Godwin left Burma in July 1853 but a strong British garrison

Field artillery outside the Great Pagoda at Prome, photographed by John MacCosh. MacCosh had begun with portrait work but during the Burma War took many views of the pagodas of both Rangoon and Prome. This scene shows field guns and Indian sepoys, detachments of whom were drawn from the Bengal and Madras presidency armies for the campaign, before two large stone dogs.

remained. The rest of Burma would fall to the British in 1886.

The war produced perhaps the first campaign photographs taken by John MacCosh, a surgeon with an artillery battery. MacCosh (1805-85) had served in both the Gwalior and Sikh wars and possibly began his photographic work in the mid 1840s.

Crimean War, 1854-6

The Ottoman Empire, 'the sick man of Europe', had survived so long largely because no European power was willing to risk facing the problems of filling the vacuum such a collapse would cause. The Dardanelles were also of considerable strategic importance to Russia and the powers endured continual crises in this sensitive area. The last crisis in 1840 had seen a temporary co-operation between Russia and Britain to save the Empire from Mehemet Ali, pasha of Egypt. But the failure of projected Turkish reforms led to revolts in the Lebanon and Bosnia, which in 1853 brought Austrian intervention to preserve Montenegro from Bosnian rebels. The submission of the Ottoman Empire to the Austrian demands at the time was noted in Russian diplomatic circles.

In the 1840s Franco-Russian tensions were increased by the dispute between the Catholic and Orthodox churches over the so-called 'holy places'. France claimed right of access and the right to repair the Church of the Holy Sepulchre under an ancient treaty of 1740 and the Russians, on rather more doubtful grounds, claimed similar rights from the 1774 Treaty of Kutchuk Kainjardi. Emperor Napoleon III, whom Tsar Nicholas I refused to recognise, found in the dispute a convenient peg upon which to hang his popularity in France. Encouraged by the Austrian success with regard to Montenegro, the Russians attempted to force concessions from the Turks on their theoretical rights of interference on religious matters. On 15th May 1853 the Porte refused Russian terms and in October 1853 Russia invaded the Danubian principalities of Moldavia and Wallachia which she had briefly occupied in 1848.

In response the British and French fleets were sent to Besika Bay, the British action being taken by Prime Minister Lord Aberdeen and Foreign Secretary Clarendon without consulting their Cabinet colleagues. Tsar Nicholas was convinced that

Lieutenant-Colonel Hallewell, 28th Foot, photographed by Fenton. To a large extent the hardship of the campaign was shared by officers and men. As a result many officers were openly critical of Raglan's handling of the campaign, and Russell and other correspondents, denied contact with headquarters, were greatly influenced by what they heard from junior officers. Edmund Gilling Hallewell had begun his career as ensign in the 20th Foot in 1839, transferring to 28th Foot while a captain in 1851. He received his majority in December 1854, becoming a lieutenant-colonel on the staff in November 1855. Hallewell became colonel in 1860 and Commandant of the Royal Military College at Sandhurst in 1863. He died in 1869.

Left: A group at headquarters, photographed by Fenton, showing General Pélissier (right), beside Lord Raglan. Raglan, though popular with the men, went to great lengths to avoid enthusiasm, and his lack of display contrasts with his French counterpart. Never having commanded even a battalion in the field, he was not forceful enough as a general. The disasters and mounting criticism wore him out, and he died on 3rd July 1855.

Below: Captain Walker reading general orders, by Fenton. Walker began his service as ensign in 30th Foot in 1846. He served as adjutant in the Crimea, being wounded at the Alma. Promoted to captain in 3rd Foot, he was severely wounded in 1855 and had his right arm amputated. He was awarded the Victoria Cross for gallantry at Inkerman in 1854, and died as General Sir Mark Walker VC in 1902.

Aberdeen would avoid war, especially as Nicholas considered he had gained Aberdeen's agreement in 1844 to partition the Ottoman Empire. Neither Aberdeen at the time nor his successors recognised any such commitment. The Russian fleet destroyed the Turkish fleet at Sinope on 30th November 1853 and Britain and France declared war on 27th March 1854. The Allies were also joined by Sardinia, anxious to gain prestige in the international arena.

Considerable difficulties were met in preparing a British Expeditionary Force of some 30,000 men which was assembled at the Dardanelles under the command of Lord Raglan in the spring of 1854. The Allies moved to Varna where in July 1854 cholera struck. It was not until 14th September that the British disembarked at the aptly named Calamita Bay, some 25 miles from the Russian base of Sebastopol. The Cabinet had ordered Raglan to besiege the city, being the most vulnerable point at which an effort could be made.

The Allied army advanced towards Sebastopol, forcing the heights above the river Alma on 20th September against the Russian army of Prince Menschikoff which streamed back into the city. Immediate pursuit and an assault upon the unprepared city was vetoed by the dying French commander-in-chief, Marshal St Arnaud. By the time the Allied army had begun their siege works the city had been ably fortified by Lieutenant Colonel Todleben, a brilliant engineer, and Vice Admiral Korniloff. The British relied upon the small port of Balaclava, seven miles from the trenches, for their supplies and this line of communication was open to Russian interference, for the British had not the troops to defend both Balaclava and the trenches. The first Russian effort on 25th October 1854 resulted in the battle of Balaclava, when the Russians almost succeeded in breaking through the weak force defending the harbour. Their second attempt at Inkerman was launched in heavy fog and drizzle on 5th November 1854 and was repulsed with heavy losses. The battle is generally called the 'Soldiers' Battle' due to the confusion and lack of higher control over the fighting. Thereafter the Russians made no concerted attempt to disrupt the line of supply.

The Allied armies before Sebastopol now found themselves at a distinct disadvantage, for the defenders of the city had ample guns, ammunition, reinforcements and supplies, their lines of communication safeguarded by Menschikoff's army. The lack of proper organisation of transport, commissariat and medical departments in the British army was soon exposed by the onset of

Remnants of the 13th Light Dragoons, the morning after the charge at Balaclava. The Light Brigade consisted the 4th and 13th Light Dragoons, 17th Lancers, 11th and 8th Hussars. Contributing factors to the disaster were the quarrel between Lord Lucan, commanding the Cavalry Division, and Lord Cardigan, commanding the Light Brigade; the cavalry's resentment at Raglan's poor handling of it; Raglan's imprecise orders given from a vantage point denied Lucan and Cardigan; and the insubordination of Captain Nolan who carried the order. Some 673 men charged into the north valley and 193 mounted men returned. The brigade lost 113 dead, 134 wounded and 475 horses killed, the 13th Light Dragoons having only ten men mounted after the charge. The Light Brigade was shattered and was of little use for the remainder of the war.

winter, heralded nine days after Inkerman by a severe storm. The snow and mud almost completely blocked the track between Balaclava and Sebastopol and while stores were heaped in complete chaos at the harbour, the men in the trenches suffered from lack of warm clothing, food and shelter. Disease was rife and the medical services broke down completely. The plight of the army, which frequently had fewer men in the trenches than the Russians behind their defences, was brought to the notice of the British public by the *Times* correspondent, W. H. Russell, and letters written home from the front. Palmerston assumed direction of affairs in February 1855 and slowly the chaos at home was overcome and proper stores, huts, equipment and reinforcements were sent to the Crimea. In March 1855 a railway was completed between Balaclava and the front line. Pélissier became French commander-in-chief in May 1855 in succession to the cautious Canrobet.

The first major assault on the Russian defences, of which the Redan and Malakoff redoubts were the prominent features, took place on 18th June 1855 and failed miserably. Lord Raglan, worn out by his command, died on 3rd July, to be replaced by General Simpson. Disease and disciplinary problems were by no means eliminated but the Russian defenders were demoralised by the wounding of Todleben in July and the defeat of a Russian force by the French and Sardinians at Tchernaya in August. On 8th September 1855 the Allies again assaulted the city. The British failed at the Redan but the French seized the Malakoff, amongst the defenders of whom was Leo Tolstoy. As a result the Russians abandoned the city destroying their defences as they retreated. Although the Treaty was not signed until March 1856 for all intents and purposes the war was over.

The Crimean War is noted for being the first conflict extensively recorded in photographs. There were some small photographic expeditions in 1854 and James Robertson, superintendent and chief engineer of the Imperial Mint at Constantinople, took photographs during the army's stay at Varna. Robertson arrived in the Crimea in September 1855 and made many studies of the results of the assaults of 9th September. Roger Fenton, the most famous of the Crimean photographers, arrived under royal

Opposite top: English infantry (3rd Buffs) piling arms, by Fenton. The British full-dress uniform was entirely unsuited to campaigning. The coatee worn here was too tight, as were the high collar and stock and equipment straps. The publicity given to the troops' suffering led to the abandonment in 1855 of the coatee for a French-style tunic. The 1844 'Albert' shako was replaced by a smaller type. The Minie rifle, a much improved muzzle loader issued only in 1854, caused severe Russian losses at Inkerman.

Opposite bottom: Men of 68th Foot in winter dress, by Fenton. The summer heat caused severe hardship to the army when they first landed in the Crimea, and winter too took its toll. Officers and men wore a variety of costumes to combat the lack of warmth, fuel and food. Clothing ignored dress regulations and officers had to wear swords to be recognised. Ironically it was the reinforcements from England who succumbed more quickly to disease. The men pictured are undoubtedly better dressed than most.

patronage in February 1855 and eventually published some 360 views and portraits. Fenton could not, of course, take any action scenes due to the long exposures but his posed portraits still manage to avoid appearing stilted. He confined himself to tasteful scenes to avoid offence and also to convince the public that things had improved since the winter.

By the Treaty of Paris, the Black Sea was neutralised, the Dardanelles were made an international waterway and the Russian protectorate over the Danubian principalities was ended. There was no real result of the war: Russia turned eastwards but repudiated the Black Sea clauses in 1870; Turkey was preserved for a future crisis. At least there was a new determination in some circles in Britain that the army would be reformed, but it had taken 21,000 dead to impress the fact that further measures were required.

Lieutenant Meecham (Hodson's Horse) and Assistant Surgeon Anderson with Sikh officers and men (photographed by Felice Beato). Hodson's Horse originated in the Punjab in 1857 and was organised at Delhi. Prompt measures on the Frontier by men such as John Lawrence, Chief Commissioner of the Punjab, John Nicholson and Neville Chamberlain prevented the spread of revolt and allowed the dispatch of columns to support the British forces in Central India and Oudh. The Sikhs proved loyal and useful allies to the British.

Indian Mutiny, 1857-8

The Indian Mutiny was an almost feudal reaction to what Indian ruling classes conceived to be a British attempt to destroy the fabric of Hindu and Moslem society which had been left undisturbed by the previous Mogul rulers of India. Lord Dalhousie, as Governor General, had pushed ahead reforms and in particular the annexation of native states where there was no direct heir and estates to which there was no apparent title to the land. Eight major states, including Oudh, totalling some 250,000 square miles had been annexed in eight years and the throne of the last Mogul Emperor, Bahadur Shah II, was itself threatened with extinction. The grievances of the dispossessed landlords and princes were spread among the Bengal army, some three-fifths of which were high-caste Brahmins and over sixty per cent from Oudh. The Bengal army, one of three presidency armies in the pay of the East India Company, was suffering from lax discipline and was susceptible to rumours of an attack upon caste by the British. In previous years some regiments had refused to serve overseas and the issue of the new Enfield cartridges, allegedly greased with pig and cow fat, was a convenient rallying point for the dissidents. It was in fact an attempt to rescue eighty-five troopers of the 3rd Bengal Light Cavalry at Meerut on 10th May 1857, where they had been imprisoned for refusing to use the cartridges, that sparked off the Mutiny.

The British had only 45,000 European troops and reinforcements took some months to arrive but fortunately the Mutiny was confined to Oudh, central India and Rohilkund; the Madras and Bombay armies did not rise. The British were also able to rely upon Sikhs and Punjabis. The main problem was to find troops for mobile columns to relieve garrisons whilst maintaining pressure against rebel centres. Fortunately Delhi became the focal point for the mutineers.

The British took up positions on the ridge at Delhi about two miles from the city but were paralysed by lack of men and the death of the Commander-in-Chief, General Anson. Cholera was rife in the stifling heat and the besiegers had only some 4,000 men and no siege artillery against 30,000 mutineers in the city. The situation was transformed by the arrival of Brigadier General John Nicholson from the Punjab who led the assault on the city on 14th September 1857. Delhi was recaptured.

Meanwhile, in June 1857 a small garrison at Cawnpore, commanded by Major General Sir Hugh Wheeler, had surrendered to Nana Sahib and had been treacherously massacred. The results of the massacre were revealed when Sir Henry Havelock and Sir James Outram, the 'Bayard of India', entered the town en route to relieve Lucknow. The Chief Commissioner of Oudh, Sir Henry Lawrence, had withdrawn into the residency at Lucknow in May and the small garrison was hard pressed by a rebel force varying from 30,000 to 100,000 men at any one time. Havelock and Outram fought their way into the town on 25th September but were too weak to evacuate. The siege was ended on 22nd November when Sir Colin Campbell, appointed Commander-in-Chief in August, relieved the town long enough to evacuate the garrison.

The turning point was reached when Campbell defeated the rebel army of Tantia Topi outside Cawnpore in December 1857. In March 1858 Campbell retook Lucknow. Meanwhile, Major General Sir Hugh Rose, with only 4,500 men, cleared central India in some sixteen actions over an area of a thousand miles, storming Jhansi on 3rd April 1858 and defeating Tantia Topi coming to the aid of the Rani of Jhansi at Kalphi on 22nd May 1858. By December 1858 the remaining mutineers had been dispersed to the borders of Nepal.

Opposite: Secundra Bagh (Alexander's Garden), Lucknow, after the slaughter of the rebels. The defenders of Lucknow had to wait a further six weeks before the Commander-in-Chief, Sir Colin Campbell, could finally evacuate the garrison. On 16th November 1857 the 93rd Highlanders, 53rd Foot and 4th Punjab Infantry (Sikhs) took Secundra Bagh, which barred their way to the Residency, after four hours of hand-to-hand fighting. Enraged by the atrocities committed at Cawnpore and elsewhere by the mutineers, the Highlanders killed approximately 1,857 rebels, according to Captain Garnet Wolseley who counted the bodies. The bones of the rebels can be seen clearly in this study by Beato, an Italian who took his photographs of Lucknow in March 1858, when Campbell returned to the city.

*The Residency at Lucknow, showing
the room in which Sir Henry Lawrence
was killed, by Beato. Lawrence had
stocked the Residency with ample
supplies at the first sign of danger. The
garrison comprised 600 men of 32nd
Foot, a company of 84th Foot, 220
volunteers, 750 loyal Indians and
1,300 civilians. On 2nd July Lawrence
was mortally wounded by a shell
bursting in his room. The defence then
devolved upon Brigadier John Inglis
until the arrival of Havelock and
Outram in September.*

*Elephant battery: siege guns at Lucknow, by Beato. When Campbell returned
to the city in March 1858 he had 400,000 men and full equipment. Elephant
batteries were operated by Royal Artillery personnel, but with Indian
mahouts riding the elephants. The photograph indicates the way in which
dress regulations were modified by the climate. Khaki had been adopted by
some regiments in India in the 1840s but this had been merely crude dyeing
of white uniforms with coffee, curry powder or mulberry juice.*

Third China War, 1860

Chinese hostility to European traders and diplomats was increasingly resented by the Powers. This culminated in 1839 in the seizing by the Chinese of large British opium stocks at Canton, the object of a profitable smuggling trade, and the expulsion of the British traders from Macao and Canton. The First China War or 'Opium War' (1840-2) was ended by the Treaty of Nanking, ceding Hong Kong to Britain and opening five ports to European trade. A comfortable indemnity was also paid for the lost opium. However, further incidents, including the execution of a French missionary and the trial for piracy of five Chinese sailors taken off the British schooner *Arrow*, led to the renewal of hostilities in 1846. The Second China War or 'Arrow War' (1846-7) resulted once more in the bombardment of Canton by a British fleet.

Negotiations following the second war led to the Treaty of Tientsin in June 1858 though the British had to seize the Taku forts at the mouth of the river Peiho to reach Tientsin. This treaty opened a further eleven ports to Europeans, allowed European missions in Peking and guaranteed the protection of missionaries and travellers in China. Admiral Hope carried the first British and French representatives to China in 1859 but his vessels were fired on from the Taku forts in June 1859 and he was unable to break through. Hope himself was wounded. This brought a renewal of war — the Third China War in 1860.

A combined British and French force numbering some 16,000 men and commanded by Lieutenant General Sir Hope Grant and General de Montauban landed at Peh-tang on 1st August 1860. The countryside had ample supplies to support the armies and use was made of a Chinese coolie corps as porters. Apart from harrying by bands of Tartar cavalry led by General San-ko-lin-sin, known to the British troops as 'Sam Collinson', the advance proceeded well through Sinho and Tang-ku which was taken on 14th August. The chief obstacles were the now familiar Taku forts which were taken by assault on 21st August 1860. Negotiations were now opened with the Chinese as the Allies advanced with the object of gaining the ratification of the Treaty of Tientsin. At Chan-chia-wan the Chinese treacherously seized Allied envoys when they went to negotiate the treaty ratification and the Allies were forced to fight a small battle and another at Pal-le-chiao. With the Allied armies before Peking, the Chinese returned the surviving diplomats on 8th October, but two had been executed and eighteen had died from maltreatment. The French had already captured and plundered the Summer Palace outside Peking and as a reprisal for the treatment of the envoys, the British burnt it to the ground on 18th October.

On 24th October 1860 the Chinese signed the Treaty of Peking ratifying the former treaty, adding Tientsin to the ports opened and ceding Kowloon to Britain on a ninety-nine year lease. Strangely, while the British were marching on Peking, they detached the 44th Foot at the request of the Imperial authorities in Shanghai to help defend the town against the Taiping rebels, a quasi-Christian sect. Charles Gordon was employed from 1860 to 1865 leading the 'Ever Victorious Army' against the rebels. No European armies set foot in China until the Boxer Revolt of 1900.

The anchorage of the British fleet at Talien-wan Bay. The photograph clearly shows the tents of the British base at Talien-wan, whence the troops were dispatched to Pehtang across the Gulf of Pechili. The British fleet proved ideal for the transport of supplies to the advancing armies, especially after the boom across the Peiho river was breached with the capture of the Taku forts. The absence of so many warships in China caused fears in Britain of inadequate naval protection in the English Channel.

The British headquarters, showing captured wooden guns, by Beato. It is not clear exactly where this photograph was taken but it is most probably in the Pehtang fort. Chinese fortifications frequently had a ramp inside leading to a raised masonry gun platform called a cavalier. The Chinese army was not well equipped, possessing only a few field pieces capable of firing at most a pound shot. The field army was mainly composed of Tartars armed with primitive matchlocks, bows and pikes.

Taku North Fort, stormed by the Allies, 21st August 1860, showing the breach and entrance effected by the troops. The Taku Forts were a formidable obstacle surrounded by ditches and chevaux de frise, as shown in this photograph by Beato. Some 2,500 British and 1,000 French troops assaulted the northernmost fort from the rear. They used scaling ladders to reach a breach made by their artillery, including new Armstrong 12pdr breechloaders. Six Victoria Crosses were won in the assault which cost the British 201 casualties (17 dead) and the French 158.

The interior of Taku North Fort immediately after capture, 21st August 1860 (photograph by Beato). Some of the damage done by the Allied artillery is clear in this scene. Note the matchlock in the immediate foreground lying by the dead Chinese. The portfires attached to the wrists of the dead were erroneously taken at the time to indicate that the Chinese had been tied to their guns to prevent flight. After the storming of the North Fort and of the second fort in line by the French, the third and final fort surrendered. The boom across the river Peiho was removed on 22nd August, and the fleet could sail once more to Tientsin.

Ambeyla Expedition, 1863

The inaccessible Mahabun Mountains were the base for a highly organised band of Hindustani fanatics who, by the late 1850s, were causing considerable trouble with incursions into the Peshawar district. A small expedition in 1852 had dispersed them for a time and in 1858 a larger expedition under Sir Sydney Cotton drové them from their base at Sitana. By 1863 the fanatics had reassembled around Malka. As a result the Lieutenant Governor of the Punjab, without the knowledge of the Commander-in-Chief, Sir Hugh Rose, authorised a punitive expedition to destroy Malka. Some 5,000 men were gathered under Brigadier General Sir Neville Chamberlain, aged only forty-three but ailing and anxious for retirement. Rose was critical of denuding the Frontier of the force especially as he considered this too small a force and too lightly equipped to achieve its object.

Chamberlain had decided to use the Chamla Valley for his base of operations and had three points of access to the valley from which to choose. His choice fell on the Ambeyla Pass when political officers assured him the local Bunerwal tribe were friendly. Chamberlain's 'Peshawar Column' set out on 19th October 1863 reaching the pass on 20th October. However, this route was harder than anticipated and the rear troops only arrived on 22nd October. Meanwhile the fanatics had convinced the Bunerwals that they should resist the British or risk annexation, and a reconnaisance patrol led by Lieutenant Colonel Probyn was attacked on 22nd October. Chamberlain's camp was on fairly level ground surrounded by rocky peaks with the Guru Mountain to one side. He decided to fortify his position and the rocky outcrops provided ideal outposts — that on the Guru mountain was called 'Eagles Nest', and that on the hills opposite 'Crag Picket'. Both these posts could contain only small numbers of men. By now the fanatics had raised all the tribes between the Indus and Kabul

rivers, totalling some 15,000 tribesmen — Chamberlain was trapped.

Fierce fighting began on 26th October and both outposts were under heavy attack. On 20th November Chamberlain was severely wounded at the Crag Picket, the same day on which the Viceroy, Lord Elgin, died in India. The Viceregal Council now wished to withdraw from Ambeyla despite Chamberlain's requests for reinforcements. Sir Hugh Rose was opposed to withdrawal and sent two aides, Colonel Adye and Major Frederick Roberts VC, to view the position. Both were in favour of continuing the campaign and Rose announced his intention of taking charge of the expedition himself. By 6th December the column, now under the command of General Garvock, had been reinforced to a total of 8,000 men, and on 15th December Garvock broke out of the pass with 4,800 men in two columns. Rose was by no means pleased with Garvock's action, which had been at the advice of his political officer.

On 17th December a Bunerwal deputation came to submit to Garvock. The expedition had proven very costly indeed with around 1,000 casualties or roughly half the casualties the British suffered in forty-two major expeditions on the Frontier between 1849 and 1890.

Opposite: Western lookout, picket and camp, Ambeyla Campaign. The difficult terrain is apparent and the men are hard to pick out. Pathans and Gurkhas proved better at picket work than Sikhs and British. (Photograph by H. Senior, 2nd Gurkhas).

Right: Camp of 3rd Sikhs, by Senior. Chamberlain's camp at the crest of the pass, amidst fir-covered peaks, was surrounded by an improvised fortification. The broken terrain enabled the tribesmen to approach unnoticed.

Officers of 12th Foot at Tauranga, September 1866 (from left to right: Captain O'Shaughnessy, Lieutenant Foster, Surgeon Manley, VC, Lieutenant Triphook and Quartermaster Laver). Two companies of 12th Foot served in the Taranaki War in 1860, the remainder of the regiment arriving in 1863. W. G. N. Manley (1831–91) won the Victoria Cross for rescuing wounded at the Gate Pa. The battalion returned to Tauranga in 1866 and established camp on a hill named Minden Peak, a reference to an earlier battle honour. They left in 1867. The town of Hamilton on the Waikato was named after their colonel.

Third Maori War, 1863-72

Trouble had begun in the North Island of New Zealand with settler pressure to purchase Maori tribal land. This culminated in the rebellion of Hone Heke from 1844 to 1846, sparked off by the cutting down of a flagpole at Kororareka, near Auckland. The fighting of the First Maori War died down reasonably quickly. However, settler pressure continued in the face of increasing Maori opposition resulting from the growth of a Maori 'king' movement in the late 1850s. This loose federation of tribes remained at peace until in 1859 Governor Gore Brown violated the principle of tribal ownership of land by purchasing an area along the Waitara river from a minor chief whom the Maoris did not regard as the rightful owner. Attempts to survey the land led to an outbreak in the Taranaki region from 1860 to 1861, the Second Maori War.

The Maoris were expert field engineers and guerrilla fighters. Their fortified stockades known as 'pas', chains of rifle pits connected by trenches and surrounded by tree-trunk palisades, were well sited and solidly constructed. The alternative to a costly frontal assault was bombardment or sapping.

The Third Maori War broke out in April 1863 following an ambush of men of the 57th Foot along the military road in the Waikato district, the construction of which was opposed by the Maoris. General Sir Duncan Cameron could only proceed as had his predecessors from pa to pa. Cameron suffered severe losses at Rangiri on 20th November 1863 but pushed ahead to occupy the Maori 'Kingite' centre of Ngaruwahia on 8th December 1863.

In 1864 Cameron captured two notable pas in the Tauranga area — the Gate Pa on 29th April and the Te Ranga Pa on 21st June, where the 43rd and 68th Foot led the assault. At Te Ranga the British were able to inflict 120 casualties upon the Maoris, normally an elusive enemy. The Maori king, Matutaera, fled into the hills for an exile of seventeen years.

No sooner had Cameron pacified Waikato than another

The Gate Pa seemed from a distance a formidable obstacle, but the palisade surrounding the maze of rifle pits and trenches was only a flimsy construction. On 29th April 1864 bombardment secured a breach and an entry was forced. Their retreat cut off, the Maoris repelled the assault, but abandoned the pa during the night.

outbreak occurred in Taranaki. This outbreak was led by a curious sect, known after their battle cry as the Hau Hau. A mixture of Christianity and Maori belief contributed to the Hau Hau faith which included the belief that they were immune to bullets. Cameron and later General Sir Trevor Chute campaigned against these fanatics who committed several atrocities of cannibalism until their demise in 1868. Another sect known as the Ringatu, led by Te Kooti, massacred some settlers at Poverty Bay on the east coast of the North Island in 1868 and were not pacified until 1872. In all, the Maori Wars between 1845 and 1872 cost the lives of 560 British and colonial troops, 250 friendly Maoris and about 2,000 hostile Maoris.

Part of the military encampment at Ngaruawahia with the gunboat 'Rangiriri' towing a barge on the Waikato river, 1863. Cameron's advance towards Ngaruawahia was supported by a flotilla of gunboats and armoured barges on the Waikato. The Royal Navy provided 200 seamen and marines for landing parties as well as performing the functions of supply and transport.

Abyssinian Expedition, 1867-8

The Christian emperor of Abyssinia, Theodore III, had successfully consolidated his control over the country by the mid 1850s. Theodore may well have begun his anti-Moslem crusade and drive for reforms with the best of intentions but his unstable character, accentuated by the death of his first wife, led to excess. In February 1862 Captain Cameron arrived as replacement for the former British consul, a firm friend of the emperor who had been killed in a skirmish. Cameron presented a pair of pistols from Queen Victoria and suggested Theodore should conclude a treaty of friendship with the Queen. Unfortunately, Theodore's letter was lost somewhere in the Foreign Office and Cameron further infuriated the emperor by visiting the Moslem Sudan in 1863 to investigate slavery and the prospects of cotton trading. Theodore imprisoned European missionaries and Cameron who had returned in January 1864. Negotiations were eventually begun by the British through an Iraqi called Rassam but he, too, was eventually confined by Theodore. The British government in 1866 had considerable problems with reform agitation, the Austro-Prussian war and a cattle plague, and it was not until August 1867 that Lord Derby finally sent an ultimatum, which was ignored.

The projected campaign posed tremendous problems of transport and supply in the mountains of Abyssinia as well as disease. It would have to be conducted in the December-June dry season and it was by no means certain that Theodore would remain at his capital of Magdala, some four hundred miles from the sea, or spare his captive at the approach of the British. The task devolved upon Lieutenant General Sir Robert Napier, Commander-in-Chief of Bombay Presidency Army since 1865. After some obstruction from Indian governmental authorities Napier assembled a force of 13,000 fighting troops (4,000 Europeans), 14,500 camp followers, scientists, 36,000 pack animals (horses, mules, camels and bullocks) and 44 elephants to carry the heavy guns. Napier was determined that the campaign should be properly organised and materials were taken for a railway, port and telegraph. In November 1867 Parliament had to pass a special vote of £2 million to cover the cost of the expedition, not least the hiring of over two hundred ships and seventy-five steamers to convey the force to Abyssinia. At least Napier had secured for himself freedom from control by the Indian establishment.

The advance party landed at the Egyptian outpost of Zula on Annesley Bay in mid October 1867, and began to construct the port, railway and a route to the mountains. Napier arrived on 2nd January 1868 and organised his force into two divisions — the 1st Division of 5,000 fighting men to advance on Magdala and the remainder in 2nd Division to hold the lines of communication. The advance began from the forward base at Senafé on 25th January. Napier met Prince Kassai, foremost of Theodore's rivals, in February. The march through the mountains and ravines made only about ten miles a day and meanwhile Theodore was moving back to Magdala with 8,000 tribesmen and several large guns built for him by German artisans. On 9th March, with Napier nearing Magdala, Theodore had six hundred natives thrown from a cliff during one of his rages. Magdala itself, standing 1,000 feet up on the plug of an extinct volcano, was virtually inaccessible.

On 10th April Napier's leading troops, led by the 4th Foot, reached the Arogee plateau below the citadel and were faced by a concerted rush by 6,500 of Theodore's tribesmen. The breech-loaders and rockets, manned by a naval party, shot down 700 and wounded 1,200 tribesmen for a British loss of twenty wounded, two of whom died later. Theodore released his prisoners on 11th and 12th April after an attempt to commit suicide had failed. The emperor expected the British to leave but his gift of cattle to Napier was refused. Theodore would not surrender and made an attempt to escape on 13th April but returned to his citadel; only a few hundred of his followers remained with him. On 13th April the 2nd Brigade led by 33rd Foot assaulted the gate of the citadel. Two Victoria Crosses were won in the assault which cost the British only fifteen wounded. When the defence collapsed Theodore shot himself with one of the pistols given him by Victoria in 1862. Napier evacuated Magdala and it was blown up on 17th April 1868.

Above: Zula Camp, photographed by 10th Company Royal Engineers. Zula, thirty miles from Massawa, was chosen as base camp because of its sheltered bay and nearness to the mountains, but intense heat and shortage of water nullified some of the advantages. The photograph shows some of the many nationalities (Indians, Persians, Egyptians, Turks, Arabs and Abyssinians) engaged in the construction work. The climate and indiscipline of the workers caused chaos until the arrival of Napier's second in command, Sir Charles Staveley, in December 1867.

Below: Camp of the 10th Company Royal Engineers at Upper Zoorru. The Zoorru Pass was the point of access to the interior and was the terminal of the railway. The 10th Company included a nine-man photographic party and was to supervise the laying of the telegraph and roads. It was involved at Arogee and led the assault on Magdala with the 33rd Foot.

Above: Royal Engineer officers in Zululand. The small garrison at Rorke's Drift heard of Isandlwana on 22nd January 1879. Available to defend the hospital and storehouse were about 140 men. The defence devolved upon Lieutenant R. E. Chard (arrowed) and Lieutenant Bromhead, 24th Foot.

Below: Rorke's Drift two weeks after the defence. A barricade was erected before the Zulus appeared. During twelve hours' desperate fighting the hospital was set alight and the defenders were forced back into their last redoubt. By 4 a. m. the Zulus withdrew, having lost 500 dead. Seventeen defenders were killed but eleven won VCs, including Chard and Bromhead.

Zulu War, 1879

The Cape route was of paramount importance to the security and commerce of Victoria's empire. The opening of the Suez Canal in 1869 by no means diminished the Cape's significance, as the Suez route might well be disrupted in any future European war. The trek of the Boers from British rule in 1835 endangered the security of the route in that Boer expansion might reach the coast or induce native unrest on the frontiers of Cape Colony. Britain therefore annexed Natal in 1843 and what would become the Orange Free State in 1847. A revulsion against expansion in Britain then led to Britain abandoning all interests in the Transvaal by the Sand River Convention of 1852 and in the Orange Free State by the Bloemfontein Convention of 1854.

The tide of imperial sentiment had revived by the 1870s and Britain annexed the newly discovered diamond fields. The Boer republics and particularly their frequent clashes with native populations still threatened the frontiers of the Cape and Natal. Lord Carnarvon, as Colonial secretary, saw the answer in federation, on the Canadian pattern, of British colonies and Boer republics, which alone could ensure peace. Major General Sir Garnet Wolseley, as Governor of Natal, secured half-hearted support from the colonists in 1875 and in April 1877 Sir Theophilius Shepstone annexed the Transvaal, bankrupt after a disastrous war with the Bapedis. With the Transvaal the British inherited a long-standing Boer border dispute with the Zulus.

The powerful Zulu nation, brought to prominence by Shaka (ruled 1810-28), numbered between 40,000 and 50,000 warriors organised in an elaborate system of regiments. Previously the British had supported Zulu claims in the border disputes and, indeed, Shepstone had crowned Shaka's nephew Cetewayo King of the Zulus in September 1873. Tensions now arose between Britain and the Zulus and border incidents increased. The new High Commissioner, Sir Bartle Frere, was convinced that Cetewayo was

Above: The saddle at Isandlwana, showing a sentry of the 2/24th Foot, a photograph taken when a burial party returned to the scene on 21st May 1879. Isandlwana had seemed a secure camp site for the central column and had not been fortified with a wagon laager to avoid the need to dismantle it. On 22nd January Chelmsford moved out on reconnaissance leaving five companies of 1st/24th and one company of 2/24th, several companies of Natal Native Contingent under Lieutenant-Colonel Pulleine, though Colonel Anthony Durnford soon arrived with more natives. On the approach of the Zulus, Pulleine's force became dispersed over too wide a frontage and Durnford was isolated on the plain. Traditionally, defeat has been ascribed to the exhaustion of ammunition in the firing line and to native troops giving way but in reality it was simply a matter of pressure of superior numbers. The defenders, who made their last stand on the saddle, killed some two thousand Zulus before they were overwhelmed.

Opposite: The 91st Highlanders returning from Zululand. Reinforcements of five battalions and two cavalry regiments including the 91st were rushed from England in March 1879. The 91st participated in the relief of Pearson, under constant threat of attack at Eshowe. The relief force set out on 28th March, repulsed ten thousand Zulus on 2nd April and relieved Eshowe on 3rd April. The 91st then joined the 1st Division for the second invasion of Zululand. The regiment is seen in the home field-service dress of red tunic, blue trousers and cork helmet with white cover, and armed with the Martini Henry single-shot breechloader. Note also the pipers.

behind the various native uprisings in 1878 known as the Ninth Kaffir War. Frere determined to destroy the native threat by annexing Zululand despite the opposition of the Conservative administration of Disraeli, already faced with the Second Afghan War. On 1st December 1878 Frere presented an impossible ultimatum to Cetewayo which included the demands that a British resident should be accepted in Zululand and that the Zulu military system should be dismembered. No reply was received and hostilities commenced on 11th January 1879.

The British Commander-in-Chief, Lord Chelmsford (1810-1905), had determined upon a three-pronged advance upon Cetewayo's kraal at Ulundi. It was felt the Zulus would defend Ulundi and thus present the opportunity of destroying their army in open battle. Three columns would undertake the invasion from the Tugela, Buffalo and Blood rivers whilst two further columns remained in reserve. Cetewayo merely sent impis in the direction of each column. Chelmsford had taken a calculated risk in dividing his forces and on 22nd January 1879 the camp of the central column at Isandlwana was destroyed by 14,000 Zulus. Six companies of the 24th Foot were completely wiped out (581 men and 21 officers) and of 950 Europeans in the camp only 55 survived, including Horace Smith-Dorrien, later to command II Corps BEF in 1914. Over 500 Kaffirs also died and about 300 escaped. Two posthumous Victoria Crosses were awarded to Lieutenants Coghill and Melville for attempting to rescue the colours from the camp. Isandlwana was one of the great disasters of the Victorian army. Some 3,000 to 4,000 Zulus swept on to Rorke's Drift which was defended for twelve hours by barely 140 men. The disaster at Isandlwana isolated Colonel Pearson's column at Eshowe and Colonel Wood's column was withdrawn to Kambula.

The arrival of the first reinforcements in March enabled Chelmsford to relieve Eshowe in April. Wood's column, attempting a diversion, came near to disaster at Hlobane on 28th March, but repulsed a massed attack on Kambula on the following day. Further reinforcements arrived and Chelmsford was able to commence a second invasion against a now exhausted Zulu army. Chelmsford was determined upon a battle to retrieve his reputation and he ignored, equally, peace overtures from Cetewayo and orders from Wolseley, newly arrived in Durban to supersede him. On 4th July Chelmsford smashed 20,000 Zulus at Ulundi in only half an hour. Wolseley was left to round off the campaign and Cetewayo was captured on 27th August 1879. The Zulu power was crushed but it had cost 1,430 European lives.

Second Afghan War, 1878-80

After the disasters of the First Afghan War (1839-42) Britain had left Afghanistan to its civil wars and maintained a policy of 'masterly inactivity'. Sher Ali, who emerged as Amir in 1868, appeared well disposed towards Britain but his requests for a form of alliance were politely refused. However, by the 1870s the Russians were themselves rapidly advancing in central Asia to secure a viable frontier, and it became obvious that the Russian government had lost control of the arrogant General Kaufmann. Disraeli's Conservative ministry came to power in 1874 and the new Secretary of State, Lord Salisbury, was determined to maintain Afghanistan as a buffer against Russian encroachments. Lord Lytton was sent out as Viceroy in 1876 to re-establish the so-called 'forward policy' but Sher Ali refused any British mission in Kabul. The heightening of Anglo-Russian tensions in the 1877-8 Balkan crisis led to the sending of Indian troops to Cyprus, the dispatch of the British fleet to Besika Bay and the arrival of a Russian mission in Kabul. Lytton had decided upon the removal of Sher Ali, and, with government approval, sent an ultimatum demanding the admission of a British envoy to Kabul. No reply was received and hostilities commenced on 21st November 1878.

The plan of campaign was worked out by the Commander-in-Chief, India, Sir Frederick Haines, and Lytton's military secretary, Colonel George Colley. Three columns invaded Afghanistan — Major General Sir Donald Stewart advanced from Quetta over the Bolan Pass to Kandahar; Lieutenant General Sir Sam Browne marched through the Khyber Pass taking the fortress of Ali Masjid; Major General Frederick Roberts advanced up the Kurram Valley to threaten Kabul forcing his way over the Peiwar Kotal. Sher Ali fled leaving his son, Yakub Khan, as regent. Long negotiations resulted in the Treaty of Gandamak signed on 26th May 1879. By this, a British envoy was admitted to Kabul and some frontier districts including the Kurram Valley were ceded to Britain. British troops were withdrawn but on 3rd September

1879 the British envoy and his escort were massacred in Kabul.

Roberts, now Lieutenant General, marched on Kabul and defeated the Afghans at Charasia on 6th October, entering the city on the following day. No political solution was forthcoming and Roberts was besieged in his camp for ten days before repulsing the Afghan attack on 23rd December 1879. The British occupation continued and Abdur Rahman, a nephew of Sher Ali, was installed as Amir in July 1880. On 27th July 1880 a British force was defeated at Maiwand by Ayub Khan, a brother of Yakub Khan, and Kandahar was besieged. In one of the most celebrated episodes of Victoria's reign, Roberts marched from Kabul to Kandahar in three weeks to defeat the rebels on 1st September 1880 before Kandahar.

Much debate followed on what could be done with Afghanistan and finally, in March 1881, the British withdrew their troops. Little was gained though Abdur Rahman was to remain Amir until

Lieutenant-General Sir Sam Browne and staff, by James Burke. Browne was given command of the Peshawar Valley Field Force comprising some 16,179 officers and men. On 21st November 1878 Browne reached the fortress of Ali Masjid dominating the Khyber. A flank attack was started but the defenders fled and Browne pushed on to Jalalabad, where he heard of Sher Ali's flight to Russia. Browne had won the Victoria Cross in the Mutiny. He also lost his left arm, prompting him to devise the famous Sam Browne belt, which carried both sword and pistol.

Above: The Band of 8th Foot, by Burke. 2/8th Foot and 72nd Highlanders were Roberts's only imperial battalions.

Below: Yakub Khan's first meeting with Major Cavignari and Mr Jenkyns, near Safed Sang, 7th May 1879, by Burke. When his father fled, Yakub Khan opened negotiations, and a treaty was signed at Gandamak on 26th May. Cavignari, envoy to Kabul, was an experienced frontier political officer. On 3rd September the British mission was attacked and its defenders massacred after a gallant defence. Inside were Cavignari, Jenkyns and seventy-five men of the Corps of Guides. The surviving Guides refused to surrender and died to a man after all the Europeans were killed.

The laager and abattis at Sherpur, photographed by Burke. The deportation of Yakub Khan to India enabled a fanatical Ghazni priest, Mushki-i-Alam, to raise the tribes against the British occupation. After several actions to disperse the concentrations of tribesmen, Roberts withdrew inside the cantonment. The area was reasonably defensible though without fortifications on the north-western and eastern sides. At these exposed positions an entrenchment was thrown up using a laager of gun carriages, tiers of logs, abattis and wire entanglements (clearly shown in the photograph which was probably taken on 23rd December 1879). Some 100,000 tribesmen invested Sherpur from 10th to 23rd December when they launched a massed dawn attack. The British had warning and Roberts estimated that 3,000 Afghans were killed. In ten days the British lost only ninety-six dead and 263 wounded. The rising was crushed and Sir Donald Stewart arrived with reinforcements in May 1880.

*Frederick Roberts photographed while Quartermaster General of the Indian
Army about 1875. As such he was effectively responsible for all operational
planning and intelligence work in defence of India. He left the post in 1878
to command the Kurram Field Force in Afghanistan.*

The Noon Day Gun, Kabul, 1879.

his death in 1907 and the British did not have to enter
Afghanistan again until 1919. Roberts's reputation was made by
the march to Kandahar though it was by no means his most
difficult operation. He was made KCB and became
Commander-in-Chief of the Madras Army. If Wolseley was
increasingly becoming known as 'our only general', then Roberts
could lay claim to be 'our only other general'.

First Boer War, 1880-1

In March 1880 Sir Garnet Wolseley as High Commissioner made it clear that the independence of the Transvaal would not be restored. The Boers hoped for concessions when Gladstone's Liberal ministry took office in April 1880 but the Cabinet was split between Whigs and Radicals and none was forthcoming. Boer resentment at annexation was increased by the revenue-collecting activities of the Administrator of the Transvaal, Sir Owen Lanyon, and by the alleged indiscipline of the small British garrisons left in the country. Lanyon never realised the extent of Boer dissatisfaction and Sir George Pomeroy Colley, who succeeded Wolseley in July 1880, had other problems to consider. On 16th December 1880 the Boers proclaimed a republic. On 20th December 1880 a small column comprising 273 men of the 94th Foot under Lieutenant Colonel Anstruther was ambushed on the road to Lydenburg at Bronkhorstspruit. Fifty-seven were killed, over a hundred wounded and all the survivors captured.

The Boers could raise about 7,000 men in their loosely organised but highly mobile commandos. Colley, a leading member of the Wolseley 'ring' and a soldier of high academic ability, had under 2,000 men in Natal and no regular cavalry. The seven British garrisons in the Transvaal—Pretoria, Potchefstroom, Standerton, Lydenburg, Rustenburg, Marabastad and Wakkerstroom were promptly surrounded. Morale had sunk low with monotonous garrison duty and many of Colley's soldiers were inexperienced. It was vital to relieve the garrisons and score a decisive victory sufficient to deter any Boers from the Orange Free State or Cape Colony from joining the rebels or any native revolt. The only entry route into the Transvaal from Natal across the Drakensberg was at Laing's Nek and here the Boers entrenched.

On 28th January 1881 Colley tried a frontal assault at Laing's Nek but was repulsed, with eighty-three dead and eleven wounded. The advance of 58th and 3/60th at Laing's Nek inspired a

Tents of numbers 2 and 3 camps, Convent Redoubt, Pretoria. Boer sieges tended to be of the open blockade type with camps a few miles from the defences. Colonel Bellairs, in command of the defence at Pretoria, had less than 1,000 men. Lanyon was cut off in the town with about 1,000 natives and 1,300 women and children. The garrison was concentrated around the barracks where trenches were dug and eleven redoubts constructed.

well-known painting by Lady Butler, *Floreat Etona*, and the 58th had the distinction of being the last battalion to carry its colours into action. Reinforcements arrived in February under Brigadier General Sir Evelyn Wood including the veteran 2/60th, 92nd Highlanders and 15th Hussars. However, Colley was forced to move on 8th February to reopen communications between his camp at Mount Prospect and his base at Newcastle. At Ingogo his small column of 300 men of 3/60th and some mounted infantry were pinned down by 250 Boers and lost 150 casualties.

The Gladstone ministry was anxious to enter negotiations with the Boers and Colley was forced to halt his plans whilst terms were sent to the Boers. No reply was received and Colley went ahead with the Majuba operation on the night of 26th February. He hoped to outflank the Boer position at Laing's Nek by seizing Majuba Hill, an extinct volcano rising some 2,500 feet above the Boer camp. Seven companies or 649 men were detailed for the venture but only 354 were sent to the summit. On 27th February 1881 the force was routed and Colley killed. Evelyn Wood reached Newcastle on 4th March and on the instructions of the government entered upon an armistice on 6th March. The British garrisons were revictualled for twelve days and Wood acknowledged Transvaal self-government. The Radicals were now firmly in control of the Cabinet and the Pretoria Convention of 23rd March ended hostilities and the Boers were granted independence under the suzerainty of the Queen. Sir Frederick Roberts had been sent out with considerable reinforcements whilst the Cabinet had been set on quelling the rebellion and these arrived on 24th March. Roberts sailed home immediately.

The capitulation to the Boers was widely condemned and Majuba remained a stain on the army which many hoped to retrieve. Unfortunately the lessons to be learnt from Boer mobility and marksmanship were not sufficiently appreciated. The war cost 390 British dead and 502 wounded; the Boers lost only 100 casualties.

The survivors of Lydenburg. The inhabitants of Lydenburg remained neutral when hostilities commenced and only about eighty men were available to defend the small fort outside the town. The core of the defence devolved upon fifty-three men of the 94th Foot, mostly undesirables, commanded by Lieutenant Long and Conductor Parsons. Long's wife and the chaplain, Father Walsh, were of the utmost value in raising the defenders' spirits, especially as little confidence was placed in the twenty-two-year-old lieutenant. Long eventually went sick and Dr Farley assumed command; circumstances which, coupled with the indiscipline of the garrison, led to a series of courts martial and Long's resignation from the army. The fort, however, held out despite constant bombardment from two naval cannon. The photograph shows Long and his wife with other defenders.

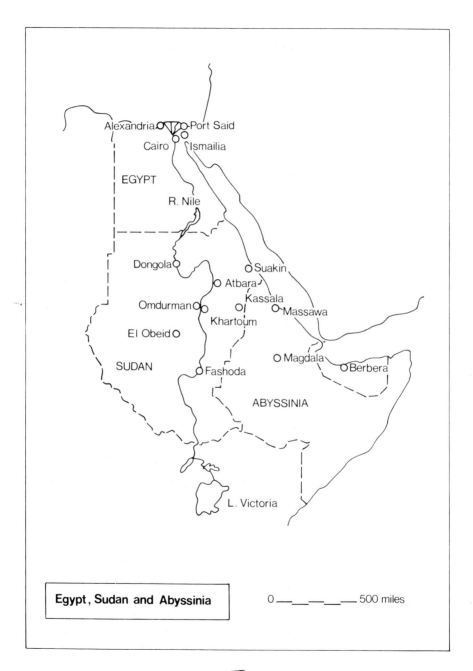

Alexandria Port Said
Cairo Ismailia

EGYPT

R. Nile

Dongola Suakin
Atbara
Kassala
Omdurman Massawa
Khartoum
El Obeid
Magdala Berbera
SUDAN Fashoda
ABYSSINIA

L. Victoria

Egypt, Sudan and Abyssinia   0 ——————— 500 miles

Egypt and the Sudan, 1882-99

It was the competition of British and French interests that brought the long British involvement in Egypt and the Sudan. Disraeli's ministry, having bought up Khedive Ismail's shares in the Suez Canal in 1875, could not permit France to extend her influence over the bankrupted Egyptian state, still nominally part of the Ottoman Empire. Thus in 1878 dual Anglo-French control was established over all Egyptian finances. This brought widespread discontent coupled with nationalist feeling against the Khedive Tewfik, which became centred on the person of Colonel Arabi who became minister of war in February 1882. The French were determined to remove Arabi but an attempt by the Khedive to dismiss him failed and led to riots in Alexandria on 11th and 12th June 1882 during which over fifty Europeans were killed. Both Whigs and Radicals in Gladstone's Cabinet wanted intervention to preserve imperial strategic and financial interests. Matters were forced by the bombardment on 11th July of newly erected Egyptian fortifications at Alexandria by Admiral Seymour who exceeded his instructions. Tewfik took refuge with the British fleet and an expedition was prepared but at this point there was a change of government in France and the French withdrew from the venture.

In a brilliant campaign, Lieutenant General Sir Garnet Wolseley landed with 35,000 men in August 1882 and smashed Arabi's army at Tel-el-Kebir on 13th September after a night march through the desert. Tewfik was restored but the British were compelled to remain to guarantee the recovery of Egyptian finances and the restoration of stable government, tasks now given to Evelyn Baring. Meanwhile, a new threat developed in the Sudan in the shape of a Sudanese revolt against corrupt Egyptian administration led by the religious fanatic known as the Mahdi. The Mahdist movement had begun in Kordofan province in 1881 and by 1882 the Mahdi had captured El Obeid. Gladstone repudiated any responsibility and eventually in 1883 an Egyptian army was dispatched under Colonel William Hicks. Hicks was annihilated south of El Obeid in November 1883. In view of the deteriorating situation in the Sudan the Government was forced to take some action but this was confined to sending out the former Governor General of the Sudan, Major General Charles Gordon, to act merely as a reporter and evacuate the Egyptian garrisons if possible. Gordon arrived at Khartoum in February 1884 just after the defeat of Valentine Baker and another Egyptian force at Tokar near Suakin by Osman Digna who had risen for the Mahdi. However, Major General Sir Gerald Graham was able to defeat Osman Digna at El Teb in March 1884 and the British remained in occupation of Suakin throughout these years.

Once in Khartoum, Gordon, Governor General once more, made no attempt to evacuate the garrisons and indulged in virtual blackmail of the government to rescue him and the Sudan. Public opinion, which had forced Gladstone to send Gordon in the first place, now demanded his relief. A relief expedition was mounted under Wolseley but was only intended to bring Gordon away from Khartoum, not to defeat the Mahdi. The campaign was mishandled and Wolseley's desert column fought two battles at Abu Klea and Abu Kru in January 1885. Steamers reached Khartoum on 28th January 1885, two days after the city had been taken and Gordon killed. The British now withdrew to Egypt speeded by the Panjdeh crisis in central Asia. The British began the reconstruction of the Egyptian army. In June 1885 the Mahdi himself died and was succeeded by the Khalifa Abdullah.

It was not until the advent of a strong Conservative ministry under Lord Salisbury in 1895 that the reconquest of the Sudan

Opposite top: Egyptian guns at Alexandria after the bombardment of 11th July 1882. This bombardment of shore batteries and defences was of the utmost interest, for there was no adequate knowledge of the effects of modern heavy naval guns upon fortifications. It was discovered that their effects in almost perfect conditions had been exaggerated and that earthworks had suffered little damage. As a result earthworks were recommended as the basis for coastal defence throughout the Empire.

Opposite bottom: Generals Valentine Baker (front centre) and Hicks (to his left) with their staffs, Cairo, 1883. William Hicks was sent by the Khedive with 10,000 Egyptian troops to hunt the Mahdi but became lost in the Kordofan. On 5th November 1883 50,000 Mahdists overwhelmed him south of El Obeid. Baker, convicted for indecent assault, was reduced to commanding the Egyptian Gendarmerie. In December he led a force to Suakin but on 4th February 1884 was routed near Tokar. Baker, unlike Hicks, escaped with his life.

Above: Scottish troops at Gizah after the battle of Tel-el-Kebir. Wolseley's route to Cairo was barred at Tel-el-Kebir by four miles of entrenchments occupied by Arabi and 26,000 of his men. On the night of 12th September 1882 Wolseley's force of 13,000 marched through the desert to deliver a surprise dawn attack on the lines. The Egyptians fled after only an hour's fighting. Cairo was occupied the following day and Arabi captured.

Opposite bottom: Highlanders burying their dead after the battle of the Atbara. The Khalifa had sent a force under the Emir Mahmud down the Nile to stem the British advance to Berber. Mahmud was entrenched on the Atbara but on 8th April 1898 Kitchener's army stormed his position, killing over 2,500 enemy for a loss of only 650 casualties. Mahmud was captured though Osman Digna, an old opponent of the British, escaped.

Opposite top: The Khalifa's army had been shattered at Omdurman with over 11,000 dead for a total British loss of 500 casualties. Gordon was avenged and on 4th September 1898 a funeral service was read at his ruined palace in Khartoum. Afterwards the British and Egyptian flags were raised from the roof and three cheers given for the Queen.

was contemplated. There was still a lingering fear of a Mahdist attempt on Egypt and new fears of French influence in the Sudan. Further, the catastrophic defeat of the Italians at Adowa in Abyssinia led to an Italian appeal for a British movement to take Mahdist pressure off their small garrison at Kassala. Major General Sir Herbert Kitchener, Sirdar of the Egyptian army, was given the task of reconquest in 1896. Two years of steady advance brought Kitchener's army to Omdurman, the Mahdist capital, across the river from Khartoum. On 2nd September 1898 Kitchener defeated the Khalifa's army before Omdurman and marched on to confront a small French force at Fashoda where it had established a fort after an epic two-year march from the French Congo. An international crisis followed until the French climbed down in December 1898.

The Khalifa remained at large and it was not until November 1899 that Sir Reginald Wingate caught and defeated the Khalifa at Um Diwaykarat. With the death of the Khalifa the Sudan was once more secure. Indeed the entire White Nile, from its source to the sea, was now under British rule; but in South Africa a new war had begun.

The Khalifa escaped from Omdurman and not until October 1899 was news received of his whereabouts. Wingate was sent after him and on 24th November found and destroyed his remaining followers at Um Diwaykarat. Among the thousand Dervish casualties was the Khalifa (the body in the foreground).

Indian Frontiers, 1883-97

After the annexation of Burma in 1886 the frontiers of India stretched for over 4,700 miles — a constant running sore to administrators and soldiers but also an unrivalled practical military training ground. When political initiatives failed to exact satisfaction for a kidnapping, murder or border raid then a punitive expedition was mounted. These operations, popularly known as 'butcher and bolt', would result in the fining or burning of a village or perhaps with withdrawal of a tribal allowance.

The Akas, one of the northern hill tribes of Assam, were a turbulent people still using bows and poisoned arrows. In 1883, due to a border dispute, they kidnapped several people, including an agent of the Calcutta Museum negotiating for exhibits. They claimed that the agent was attempting to buy their chiefs for display in the Calcutta Exhibition. The Akas refused to hand back their captives and a small expedition had to be sent to secure the release of those abducted.

The Black Mountain Tribes along the left bank of the Indus on the North West Frontier had been troublesome for some time when on 18th June 1888 they attacked a small British party on a route march and killed two British officers. The Punjab government authorised the dispatch of the Hazara Field Force under Brigadier General Sir John McQueen but severely restricted the scope of the operation. After six weeks and minimal casualties the troops were withdrawn with little impression being made on the tribes. The British did secure a promise from the tribes that British troops would be allowed to march without harassment along the crest of the Black Mountain. However, in 1890 a route march led by McQueen was obstructed and in 1891 a much larger expedition was assembled under Major General Sir William Elles. There was little hard fighting but British forces remained long enough to compel the tribes to come to terms and did not withdraw until a special border police was established in

November 1891.

Hard on the heels of the Black Mountain Expedition came trouble in the petty state of Manipur on the borders of Assam. The British had attempted to remove from office the Senapati (the local state force's commander) after he had engineered a palace revolution. As a result of this attempt the Chief Commissioner of Assam, Mr Quinton, his military commander, Colonel Skene, and three other British officers were murdered on 24th March 1891. Three columns totalling almost 5,000 men advanced from Kohima, Cachar and Tanu in early April, converging on Manipur on 27th April 1891. The murderers were brought to justice and the state declared forfeit to the Crown though it was subsequently restored to a five-year-old boy.

In 1895 the British became involved in the civil strife for the succession to the small mountain state of Chitral, some two hundred miles from Peshawar. In January 1895 the Mehtar, or ruler, was murdered by his half-brother, Amir-ul-Mulk. At this point an uncle of the murdered ruler invaded the state in co-operation with Umra Khan of Jundal, a neighbouring Pathan state. A small garrison was cut off in Chitral fort, under Surgeon Major Scott Robertson and Captain Charles Townsend, and another small garrison at Mastuj. The 1st Division under Sir Robert Low advanced from Peshawar forcing its way over the unknown Malakand Pass and the Swat and Panjkora rivers. But the garrison was relieved by Colonel Kelly and his 32nd Pioneers

Opposite top: Signallers of the Buffs, Manipur Expedition, 1891. The most celebrated exploit of the Manipur Expedition was the advance of Lieutenant Grant of the 2nd Burma Infantry from Tanu in Burma to Thobal in fourteen days with only eighty-four men, in an attempt to rescue any captives. Grant won the Victoria Cross for his action. These men of the Buffs are equipped with the heliograph, developed around the 1860s, which transmitted messages in Morse by reflecting the rays of the sun in a mirror. It needed clear visibility for ideal use and was therefore well suited to Indian conditions.

Opposite bottom: 2nd Seaforth Highlanders on Diliari Heights, Black Mountain, 1891. The force of Major-General Elles comprised two columns, the Seaforth Highlanders and the 1st Battalion Royal Welch Fusiliers being the only British battalions. The Diliari Heights were taken on 23rd March 1891 when it was realised that no commanding positions could be allowed to remain in the hands of the tribesmen. The only serious fighting was a night attack made on the 4th Sikhs.

advancing over snow-blocked mountains from Gilgit, 220 miles to the east of Chitral.

A permanent post was established at Chitral and in the Malakand but such 'forward policy' was galling to the tribes of the frontier. In 1897 a fanatic known to the British as the 'Mad Mullah of Swat' was able to raise the tribes against the British. The Turks, recently involved in war with Greece, and the Afghans also had agents on the Frontier spreading rumours and subversion. On 26th July 1897 the Malakand was attacked but its garrison held off several thousand tribesmen until relieved by Sir Bindon Blood. But the revolt spread throughout the North West Frontier and on 25th August the Khyber garrisons were overwhelmed. Expeditions had to be mounted against the Mohmands, the Orakzais and the Afridis of the Tirah Valley. Sir William Lockhart led two divisions into the Tirah and stormed the Afridi position at Dargai on 18th October 1897. By the end of the year the great Pathan rising was at an end.

Panorama from Camp Sherkhel, Bara Valley, showing an Afridi village burning, Tirah Expeditionary Force, 1897. The most famous episode of Sir William Lockhart's advance into the Tirah was the storming of Dargai Heights on 20th October 1897 by Colonel Kempster's 3rd Brigade. Piper Findlater of the Gordon Highlanders won the Victoria Cross by playing his pipes to urge the men on, though himself wounded. The fighting in the Bara Valley which followed was particularly hard, with continual attacks on the flanks and rear of the 2nd Division which retreated down it in December 1897.

Third Ashanti War, 1895-6

With the end of the slave trade only Britain remained sufficiently interested in the Gold Coast to maintain her forts and, indeed, take over those of the Danes in 1850 and those of the Dutch in 1872, when those powers abandoned their interest. The extension of British control brought conflict with the powerful inland state of Ashanti with which the British had maintained uneasy relations since a treaty of 1831, following an earlier war. In the early 1870s the Ashanti overran the buffer Fanti states leading to an expedition led by Major General Sir Garnet Wolseley in 1873-4 to Kumasi. After a model campaign Wolseley imposed an indemnity on King Kofi Karikari and demanded the end of human sacrifices in Ashanti. At the same time the Gold Coast was officially annexed as a colony.

Relations were uneventful until in 1890 the British government decided it would be wise to extend a protectorate over Ashanti in view of French colonial activities. King Prempeh declined the offer and the British revived the matter of the unpaid indemnity and continuing human sacrifice. Prempeh decided to submit but the emissary dispatched to London was too late to stop the march of a hastily organised British expedition among whom was Victoria's son-in-law, Prince Henry of Battenburg, who died from disease during the campaign.

The expedition commanded by Colonel Sir Francis Scott, Inspector General of the Gold Coast Constabulary, arrived at Cape Coast in December and reached Kumasi on 17th January 1896 without firing a shot. Prempeh proved obstinate and when the expedition departed on 22nd January for the coast, the king and other members of his household went with it as prisoners. The protectorate was established and a resident set up in Kumasi.

The Golden Stool, symbol of Ashanti kingship, had been hidden when the British arrived in 1896 and the attempts of the Governor, Sir Frederick Hodgson, to find it led to his being besieged in Kumasi in 1900. Two small columns fought their way in but in June 1900 Hodgson decided to fight his way back to the coast. The result was the complete annexation of Ashanti.

Troops landing at Cape Coast Castle, Ashanti War, 1895–6. The surf at Cape Coast Castle was notorious and all supplies and men had to be brought ashore in small boats. The expedition comprised a Special Service Corps raised from several regiments and the West Yorkshire Regiment, diverted on its way home from Aden. Colonel Scott had wanted a West India regiment and indeed the main problem was disease. There was no fighting at all, though there were occasional false alarms.

South African War, 1899-1902

After the First Boer War it seemed as if the Transvaal would, once more, slide into bankruptcy and the British in ratifying the peace terms at the 1884 London Convention omitted to confirm the suzerainty under which the Boers had been granted self-rule in 1881. The situation was transformed by the discovery of gold on the Witwatersrand in 1886 bringing the influx of many thousands of foreigners, or 'Uitlanders', mainly British. The possible effect of this 'invasion' upon Afrikaner society aroused considerable suspicions amongst the Boer population and Kruger, President of the Transvaal since 1883, was determined that they should not receive civil rights, notably the franchise which could overthrow Boer supremacy.

This coincided with the extension of British influence throughout southern Africa as part of a 'scramble for Africa' between the Great Powers. Britain annexed Pondoland in 1884, Bechuanaland in 1885 and Zululand in 1887, all of which seemed to restrict Kruger's own dreams of expansion. The creation of Cecil Rhodes's British South Africa Company in 1889 and Rhodes's immediate ambition to see a route from the Cape to Cairo entirely in British hands led to the annexation by Rhodes of Mashonaland and Matabeleland (Rhodesia) in the 1890s, further forestalling Kruger.

A revolt was planned by the Uitlanders with the support of Rhodes and the knowledge of the British Colonial Secretary, Joseph Chamberlain. However, the Venezuelan dispute between Britain and the United States caused a temporary internal dissension within the Uitlanders' ranks and no uprising took place. At this point Dr Jameson, Rhodes's administrator of Rhodesia, invaded the Transvaal from Bechunanaland with 470 police on 29th December 1895. The Jameson Raid was a foolhardy venture without Uitlander support and the force was surrounded near Johannesburg on 2nd January 1896. The repercussions were serious. Rhodes was forced to resign as premier of the Cape Colony, and throughout southern Africa Boer opinion was inflamed against what was regarded as a plot by the British Government, though Chamberlain had no knowledge of the raid. The support of the Cape Dutch was lost and the Orange Free State concluded a defensive agreement with the Transvaal.

Sir Alfred Milner was now sent out as High Commissioner with the mission to attempt to restore the imperial position in South Africa. But, while Chamberlain was now anxious to tread carefully, Milner was determined to manoeuvre Kruger into conflict. In December 1898 an Englishman was shot by a Boer policeman and over 21,000 Uitlanders petitioned the Queen for aid. Milner lent his full support to the claims upon the British government. If the government now neglected to aid the Uitlanders they risked the end of British supremacy in South Africa and the Cabinet reluctantly acknowledged that they must intervene to restore that supremacy. Milner's negotiations with the Boer leaders began at Bloemfontein in May 1899 but all efforts to reach a compromise failed due to the hard-line attitude of both sides. Having waited for the grass to grow fully on the veldt, Kruger issued an ultimatum on 9th October 1899 demanding the withdrawal of British troops from the frontier, the withdrawal of all reinforcements landed since June and the recall of troops on their way to Africa. On 11th October Boer commandos invaded Natal and Cape Colony.

For all the obvious warnings of an approaching conflict the British government made singularly little preparation for war. Only on 8th September was it resolved to reinforce Natal from India and full mobilisation in England was not ordered until 7th October. The Boers speedily invested Cecil Rhodes in Kimberley, defended by Colonel Kekewich; and Mafeking, defended by Colonel Baden-Powell, but this repeat of their 1881 tactics served to dilute their strength. Sir George White, sent from India, was able to gain some successes at Talana and Elandslaagte but was driven back into Ladysmith. The task of relieving the garrison now devolved upon the newly arrived Commander-in-Chief, Sir Redvers Buller. Buller planned to relieve White while Major General Methuen moved on Kimberley and Major General Gatacre kept the Boers occupied. The result was disaster. On 10th December Gatacre was defeated at Stormberg; on 11th December Methuen, already worsted at Modder River, was defeated at Magersfontein and finally, on 15th December, Buller was defeated at Colenso. As a result of 'Black Week', Field Marshal Lord Roberts was appointed Commander-in-Chief on 17th December with Kitchener as his Chief of Staff.

Before Roberts could begin his advance, Buller failed at Spion

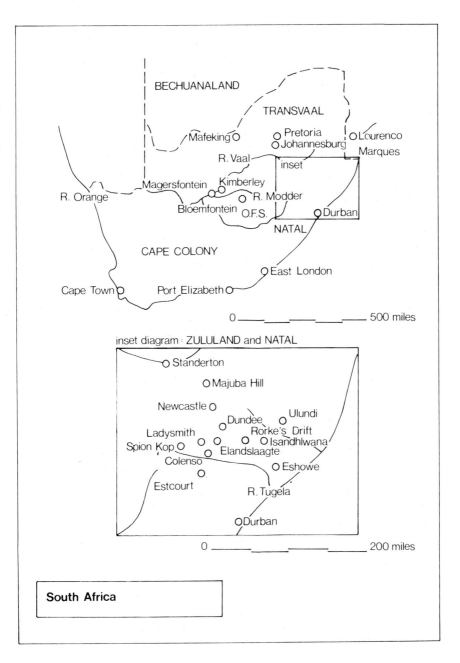

BECHUANALAND

TRANSVAAL

Mafeking O

Pretoria O
Johannesburg O

O Lourenco
Marques

R. Vaal

inset

R. Orange

Magersfontein

Kimberley

R. Modder

Bloemfontein   O.F.S.

O Durban

NATAL

CAPE COLONY

O East London

Cape Town O   Port Elizabeth O

0 _____ 500 miles

inset diagram : ZULULAND and NATAL

O Standerton

O Majuba Hill

Newcastle O

Dundee O

O Ulundi

Rorke's Drift

Ladysmith

O Isandhlwana

Spion Kop O   O   O

O Elandslaagte

Colenso O

O Eshowe

Estcourt

R. Tugela

O Durban

0 _____ 200 miles

South Africa

Kop to break through to Ladysmith though White had beaten
back a major Boer attack at Wagon Hill on 6th January 1900.
Roberts now planned to advance on Kimberley and outflank the
Boer Free State capital of Bloemfontein from the west. The
advance began on 10th February, Kimberley was relieved on 15th
February and the Boer leader Cronje surrounded at Paardeberg.
During a temporary illness of Roberts, Kitchener attacked the
Boer position on 18th February but failed. However, Cronje
surrendered 4,000 men on 27th February 1900. The next stage of
Roberts's campaign took him to Bloemfontein on 13th March.
From there, after a halt of six weeks to reorganise, Roberts
advanced on Pretoria which was captured on 5th June 1900. After
attempting to contain the talented Boer leader, de Wet, Roberts
advanced to Komati Poort on the border of Portuguese East
Africa, to cut off the main Boer outlet to European assistance.
This was captured on 24th September: Kruger had already fled to
Holland. With the war seemingly at an end Roberts handed over
the command to Kitchener on 29th November 1900 returning
home to supersede Wolseley as Commander-in-Chief.

The war, however, was far from over. Kitchener had to combat
continuing guerrilla warfare by such leaders as de la Rey, de Wet,
Smuts and Botha. President Steyn of the Orange Free State was
still at large and continued to encourage resistance as did Kruger's
deputy, Burger. Kitchener eventually beat Boer mobility by
constructing blockhouses linked by wire; by constant columns
driving across the veldt in search of the enemy, a task in which the
value of mounted infantry soon became apparent; by burning Boer
farms and seizing livestock; by detaining the guerrillas' families in
special camps. The Boers frequently scored successes over the
columns but on 30th May 1902 finally signed the Treaty of
Vereeniging. The peace held out the promise of eventual
self-government for the Transvaal and Orange Free State and
indeed this came in 1907. The terms granted the Boers were
generous and included a considerable grant to compensate for the
destruction of Boer property in the latter stages of the war.

The Boer War cost Britain almost 51,000 casualties and over
£222 million; the Boers lost about 14,000 dead. Over 450,000
British and Dominion troops were used in South Africa and the
military connections forged with the dominions were to prove of
great value in the future. The war induced much needed
administrative reforms and in one respect there was considerable
improvement — the BEF in 1914 was to astonish the Germans
with its fieldcraft and accurate rifle fire.

Above: Digging a trench at Elandslaagte. The Boer invasion of Natal was led by General Joubert. Despite a tactical victory at Talana Hill the British had to abandon Dundee. General French beat back the Boers from Elandslaagte station on 21st October 1899 but this too had to be abandoned. Sir George White remained at Ladysmith with 12,000 men to prevent intrusion into southern Natal and destruction of the vast supply dumps.

Below: Soldiers around cooking fires, Ladysmith. Lieutenant-General Sir George White was surrounded in Ladysmith by 20,000 Boers in November 1899. The Boers bombarded the town daily but it was later calculated that for each defender killed 375 shells were fired. Two major sorties were made against Boer artillery positions. Despite declining morale White refused to surrender and was finally relieved on 28th February 1900. Some 785 defenders died, 500 from disease.

*Above: Baden-Powell (extreme left) and the Mafeking Wolf Gun. Mafeking
and its small garrison of 1,200 volunteers and police was besieged from 13th
October 1899 to 17th May 1900, when it was relieved by Brigadier-General
Plumer. The garrison was not closely invested and the whole siege had almost
a carnival atmosphere. Baden-Powell possessed little artillery and many guns
were improvised. The Wolf Gun shown here was a 4½-inch howitzer made
from a drainpipe by Major Panzera; it fired cannonballs made at an
improvised blast furnace. The nickname 'Wolf' was given to Baden-Powell by
the natives and the gun was pictured on banknotes issued during the siege.*

*Opposite bottom: British troops watching the battle of Colenso, 15th
December 1899, by Barnett and Co. Buller's orders for his three-pronged
advance across the Tugela were rather vague and Colonel Long advanced
unsupported in the centre with two field batteries to within 700 yards of the
Boers. The gunners being forced to take cover, Buller, injured by a shell,
ordered the rescue of the guns. Four VCs were won in retrieving two guns,
one posthumously awarded to Lord Roberts's son. Buller now called off the
battle, though the centre attack was taking effect, and abandoned the ten
remaining guns. The British suffered a thousand casualties, the Boers lost just
six dead and twenty-one wounded.*

Right: Royal Scots Fusiliers (21st) in a trench at Mooi River, December 1899. The Mooi River camp was one of the advanced outposts of Buller's army near to Estcourt. Before Buller made his attempt to cross the Tugela at Colenso disaster had already overtaken General Gatacre and Lord Methuen. Lacking accurate topographical information Methuen had run into 6,000 Boers concealed in trenches at the Modder River on 28th November and again suffered severe losses in a dawn attack on a heavily entrenched position at Magersfontein. Gatacre tried to surprise the Boers by a night march on their position at Stormberg on 10th December but lost over a hundred casualties and six hundred captured.

*Above: In the firing line with the Wiltshire Regiment, Norvals Pont.
Major-General French operated around the area of Colesburg in December
1899 and was joined there by the Wiltshires as part of Major-General
Clement's brigade. French was given command of the Cavalry Division for the
relief of Kimberley and entered the town on 15th February 1900, having
ridden through eight hundred Boers barring the route that morning. French's
reputation was made by the relief of Kimberley.*

*Opposite: British dead at Spion Kop, Natal, 26th January 1900. Buller sent
Lieutenant-General Warren on a flanking attack across the Tugela though he
continued to interfere in Warren's plans and eventually placed Major-General
Woodgate in command of an attack upon the unmapped Spion Kop, an oddly
shaped hill rising some 1,400 feet above the Tugela. Woodgate's force climbed
the hill on the night of 23rd January 1900, but fog obscured the contours
and dawn revealed the Boers overlooking the British. Woodgate was killed and
Warren gave the command to Colonel Thorneycroft though General Coke was
also on the mountain. Weather interrupted heliograph communications and
throughout the day the commanders issued conflicting orders. The hill was
abandoned on the night of 24th January. Boer marksmen had had
commanding views of the British positions and in one place, seen here, some
seventy men were shot dead, in each case through the head.*

Above: The Royal Canadian Regiment crossing Paardeberg Drift, following the 82nd Battery Royal Artillery. The Royal Canadian Regiment had been raised from the pick of Canada's militia regiments and was commanded by Colonel W. D. Otter. Seen here crossing the river by means of ropes, the regiment comprised part of Horace Smith-Dorrien's 19th Brigade. On 26th–27th February 1900 they led a night attack on Cronje's laager on the anniversary of Majuba. They lost thirteen dead and thirty wounded in the assault but gained an enfilading position which caused Cronje to surrender the same day.

Opposite bottom: 82nd Battery on the move at Paardeberg, with five horses down in one team being unhooked under fire. On 18th February 1900 Kitchener directed the attack on Cronje's surrounded laager at Paardeberg, though he was junior to both divisional commanders present. Considerable confusion reigned throughout the day and the unco-ordinated attacks were defeated in detail. Kitchener at least succeeded in destroying Cronje's mobility by killing his oxen and horses by shell fire. However, the British lost 1,200 casualties and Roberts, on resuming command, decided to starve out the Boers.

Right: Armoured trains were a feature of the Boer War though at first, when used for reconnaissance, they often proved ineffective, being tied to a static line. They were relatively easy to disable – by destroying the lines. Railways were vital for British supplies and armoured trains, armed with a small gun, served in Kitchener's drive against guerillas.

Overleaf: The entry of British troops into Johannesburg, by Barnett and Co. During the advance on Pretoria Johannesburg was surrounded on 30th May 1900 and formally entered next day. The Boers were given time to withdraw to prevent street fighting, but large stocks of supplies were captured. On 6th June Roberts entered Pretoria and released 3,352 British prisoners.

Tibet, 1903-4

The ill-defined borders of Tibet had been a source of friction between Tibet and Britain since the 1880s and the Tibetans had never subscribed to the 1890 convention and 1893 trade regulations on the Sikkim-Tibet border concluded between Britain and China, Tibet's nominal overlord. Two letters from the Viceroy of India, Lord Curzon, to the Dalai Lama in 1900 and 1901 had failed to reach their destination and incidents continued. But the disputes on demarcation and trade were dwarfed by the fear of a possible extension of Russian influence into Tibet, from whence Russian agents could cause serious mischief on the north-eastern frontier of India. Both the arch-imperialist Curzon and the British Cabinet were ready to believe rumours of activity by Russian agents and of a secret Chinese agreement to cede their interest in Tibet to Russia. To settle the border issue and to forestall Russia in the apparent extension of the 'great game' of the North-western Frontier, Curzon despatched a commercial mission with a military escort under Colonel Francis Younghusband to negotiate with Chinese and Tibetan representatives at Khamba Jong in July 1903. In the face of a Tibetan refusal to negotiate Curzon secured Cabinet agreement for an advance to Gyantse, some 200 hundred miles from Lhasa, to force Tibetan co-operation.

The mission and escort totalling some 1,150 fighting men assembled at Siliguri in Sikkim, some four hundred miles from Lhasa, and crossed the 14,800-foot Jelap La into Tibet on 12th December 1903. A forward base was established at Tanu but the military commander, Brigadier General MacDonald, refused to winter there and the advance did not resume until March 1904. On 31st March 1904 a 1,500-strong Tibetan force blocking the road at Guru was dispersed with over 600 dead when the Tibetans resisted attempts to disarm them. The force pushed its way through the 'Red Idol' Gorge and entered Gyantse on 11th April 1904 to find its fortress or 'Jong' abandoned. It was decided to push on to

Lhasa and the British camped at the nearby Chang Lo to await reinforcements.

By the end of May a Tibetan force of some 16,000 men had invested Chang Lo despite a successful attack on the Karo La on 6th May to try to disperse the enemy. Reinforcements arrived in June and on 6th July the British stormed the Gyantse Jong. The advance was resumed and Lhasa reached on 2nd August 1904. It became obvious that the Cabinet had no clear idea of what to do with Lhasa occupied and it was left to Younghusband to negotiate a treaty before the health of his troops suffered or the passes back to India became blocked with snow.

The Tibetans agreed to recognise the 1890 convention and the 1893 trade regulations and also not to enter into dealings with any foreign power without British consent. Younghusband also imposed an indemnity to be repaid over seventy-five years with the occupation of the Chumbi Valley as security on repayment. He also negotiated for the right of any British envoy to go to Lhasa. The indemnity and the Chumbi occupation found little favour with the British Cabinet but Younghusband left Lhasa on 23rd September 1904 without renegotiating his hard won treaty. Subsequently the Chinese paid off a much reduced indemnity and extended their own interest over Tibet which Britain formally acknowledged in 1906.

In a fast-changing world, Younghusband's mission was seen as the last of its type — the swansong of the great Victorian imperial adventure.

Previous pages: Crossing the Jelap La Pass at 14,800 feet. The mission was supported by over 10,000 coolies and 19,000 pack animals including some 4,500 yaks most of which perished on the march from cold and disease. The troops were operating mostly over 14,000 feet above sea level and special warm clothing of sheepskins, quilted overalls and goggles were issued. The water in the machine guns froze and had to be replaced by a mixture of water, rum and kerosene and rifles were left unlubricated. The supply columns were frequently overtaken by blizzards.

Opposite below: Troops marching into camp at Lhasa, 3rd August 1904. The 'Forbidden City' of Lhasa was an irresistible magnet for the troops on the expedition and there was keen competition to accompany the last push on the city from Gyantse and then to be the first to sight the city. The force halted within sight of the roofs of the Dalai Lama's palace, or Potala, on 2nd August and moved in on 3rd August 1904. The need of warm clothing and the fears that snow would block the passes brought evacuation on 23rd September and the return through blizzards to Sikkim.

Above: View from the hills behind the Gyantse Jong, taken during reconnaissance on 7th July 1904, the morning after the capture of the Jong, and showing the 40th Pathans waiting outside the town for the order to enter and search it. The Gyantse Jong rose 500 feet above the surrounding plain at a height of 13,000 feet above sea level. The British did not occupy the massive fortress because of the difficulty of water supply but consequently had to retake it on 6th July 1904. A breach was made in the walls and the Tibetan magazine blew up allowing the assault party to fight its way in.

Further reading

The best secondary sources for the Victorian colonial campaigns are the official or semi-official histories produced by the War Office. Some of these have now been reprinted but as many are still only available in major reference libraries this bibliography is confined to those works most readily accessible to the general reader. Similarly, much of the most recent scholarly research is to be found in journal articles or doctoral dissertations. For some indication of such research the best guides are Hew Strachan 'Recent Writing Reviewed: The British Army, 1815-1856' and Edward Spiers 'Recent Writing Reviewed: The British Army, 1856-1914' in the *Journal of the Society for Army Historical Research* LXIII, 254 and 256, 1985, pages 68-79 and 194-207 respectively. The best synthesis for the whole period is Edward Spiers *The Army and Society, 1815-1914* (Longman, 1980) and for the late Victorian period, the same author's *The Late Victorian Army, 1868-1902* (Manchester University Press, 1992).

On Victorian campaigning the best survey remains Brian Bond (editor) *Victorian Military Campaigns* (Hutchinson, 1967), while there are now a number of books which deal with campaigns in a particular locality over a wide time scale. Among these can be counted H.C.B. Cook *The Sikh Wars* (Leo Cooper, 1975); Tom Gibson *The Maori Wars* (Leo Cooper, 1974); Michael Barthorp *To Face the Daring Maoris* (Hodder and Stoughton, 1979); Tony Heathcote *The Afghan Wars, 1839-1919* (Osprey, 1980); Edgar Holt *The Opium Wars of China* (Putnam, 1964); Alan Lloyd *The Drums of Kumasi* (Longman, 1964), A. J. Smithers *The Kaffir Wars, 1779-1877* (Leo Cooper, 1973), John Milton *The Edges of War: A History of Frontier Warfare, 1702-1878* (Cape Town, 1983), and Michael Barthorp *War on the Nile* (Blandford, 1984). An interesting approach has been that of Frank Emery, whose compilation of mostly ordinary private soldiers' letters *The Red Soldier* (Hodder and Stoughton, 1977) dealing with the Zulu War, has been followed by a general survey of campaigns in Africa *Marching over Africa* (Hodder and Stoughton, 1986). Another recent popular survey is Ian Knight *Go to Your God Like a Soldier* (Greenhill, 1996) while colonial campaigns are dealt with comprehensively in Philip Haythornthwaite *The Colonial Wars Source Book* (Arms and Armour Press, 1995).

On the administrative and domestic side of the army there has been an enormous growth of published work in recent years. For the pre-Crimean army see Hew Strachan *Wellington's Legacy, The Reform of the British Army, 1830-1854* (Manchester University Press, 1984) and the same author's *From Waterloo to Balaclava: Tactics, Technology and the British Army, 1815-1854* (Cambridge University Press, 1985). By way of contrast see John Sweetman

War and Administration: The Significance of the Crimean War for the British Army (Scottish Academic Press, 1984). Other works looking at later administration are W. S. Hamer *The British Army: Civil-Military Relations, 1885-1905* (Oxford University Press, 1970) and Ian Beckett and John Gooch (editors) *Politicians and Defence: Studies in the Formulation of British Defence Policy, 1846-1970* (Manchester University Press, 1981). Some of the older works on defence planning at the end of the Victorian period are still of value, including N. H. Gibbs *The Origins of Imperial Defence* (Oxford University Press, 1955); J. Ehrman *Cabinet Government and War* (Cambridge University Press, 1958) and F. A. Johnson *Defence by Committee* (Oxford University Press, 1960). However, more modern works have refined much of the ground, including John Gooch *The Plans of War* (Routledge and Kegan Paul, 1974); Nicholas D'Ombrain *War Machinery and High Policy* (Oxford University Press, 1973) and David French *British Economic and Strategic Planning* (Allen and Unwin, 1982). Still unsurpassed in their particular fields are Jay Luvaas *The Education of an Army* (Cassell, 1964) and Brian Bond *The Victorian Army and the Staff College* (Eyre Methuen, 1972). A more recent work of great value is T. G. Fergusson *British Military Intelligence, 1870-1914* (Arms and Armour Press, 1984). On recruitment and conditions of service, there is the superb A. R. Skelley *The Victorian Army at Home* (Croom Helm, 1977) while, despite the title, officers are the subject of G. Harries-Jenkins *The Army in Victorian Society* (Routledge and Kegan Paul, 1977).

On personalities, the best biography of Roberts is still David James *The Life of Lord Roberts* (Hollis and Carter, 1954) although it now requires revision, some aspects of which are indicated in Brian Robson *Roberts in India: The Military Papers of Field Marshal Lord Roberts, 1876-93* (Army Records Society, 1993). Wolseley's career has been covered by Joseph Lehmann *All Sir Garnet* (Cape, 1964). Adrian Preston's more critical approach can be traced in his editions of Wolseley's campaign journals: *In Relief of Gordon* (Hutchinson, 1967); *The South African Diaries of Sir Garnet Wolseley, Natal, 1875* (Balkema, Cape Town, 1971) and *The South African Journal of Sir Garnet Wolseley, 1879-1880* (Balkema, Cape Town, 1973). Kitchener has attracted much recent interest but the best biographies are Philip Magnus *Kitchener: Portrait of an Imperialist* (Murray, 1958) and George Cassar *Kitchener: Architect of Victory* (William Kimber, 1977).

The Crimean War was the first to attract a revival of interest. Cecil Woodham-Smith *The Reason Why* (Constable, 1953) is justly regarded as a classic piece of writing but it is now seen to be flawed and the work of both Strachan and Sweetman, already mentioned, provides a salutary corrective. Moreover, the wider aspects of the war, which also included campaigns in the Baltic and Asia Minor, are well covered in Andrew Lambert *The Crimean War: British Grand Strategy against Russia, 1853-56* (Manchester University Press, 1990).

Other accounts of the Crimea are Christopher Hibbert *The Destruction of Lord Raglan* (Longman, 1961) and A. J. Barker *The Vain Glorious War* (Weidenfeld and Nicolson, 1970) while a different perspective is provided by Albert Seaton *The Crimean War: A Russian Chronicle* (Batsford, 1977). The impact on Britain is the subject of Olive Anderson *A Liberal State at War* (Macmillan, 1967) but this, too, now needs reading in the context of the work of Strachan and Sweetman.

The Indian Mutiny is well covered by Michael Edwardes *Red Year* (Hamish Hamilton, 1975) and he also wrote a fine account of the siege of Lucknow, *A Season in Hell* (Hamish Hamilton, 1973). Other accounts include Christopher Hibbert *The Great Mutiny* (Allen Lane, 1978), P. J. O. Taylor *A Companion to the Indian Mutiny of 1857* (Oxford University Press, 1996), Andrew Ward *Our Bones are Scattered* (John Murray, 1996), and Alexander Llewellyn *The Siege of Delhi* (Macdonald and Jane's, 1977). For the North West Frontier see Arthur Swinson *North West Frontier* (Hutchinson, 1967) and J. G. Elliott *The Frontier, 1839-1947* (Cassell, 1968) while a good account of Chitral in 1895 is provided by John Harris *Much Sounding of Bugles* (Hutchinson, 1975) and the frontier rising of 1897 in Michael Barthorp *The Frontier Ablaze* (Windrow and Greene, 1996). The First Afghan War is covered by J. A. Norris *The First Afghan War* (Cambridge University Press, 1967) and Patrick Macrory *Signal Catastrophe* (Hodder and Stoughton, 1966) while other campaigns on the sub-continent are the subject of Barbara English *John Company's Last War* (Collins, 1971); A. T. Q. Stewart *The Pagoda War* (Faber and Faber, 1972) and the excellent account of the Second Afghan War, Brian Robson *The Road to Kabul* (Arms and Armour Press, 1986). For the Indian Army generally see Tony Heathcote *The Indian Army, 1822-1922* (David and Charles, 1972), and the same author's *The Military in British India* (Manchester University Press, 1995), Philip Mason *A Matter of Honour* (Cape, 1974) and David Omissi *The Sepoy and the Raj: The Indian Army, 1860-1940* (Macmillan, 1994).

Canada is covered by G. F. G. Stanley *Canada's Soldiers* (Macmillan of Canada, 1960); C. P. Stacey *Canada and the British Army, 1846-71* (University of Toronto Press, 1963), Desmond Morton *Canada and War* (Toronto, 1981), Elinor Senior *Redcoats and Patriots* (Canadian War Museum, 1985), Mary Fryer *Volunteers and Redcoats* (Dundurn Press, 1987), G. F. G. Stanley, *Toil and Trouble* (Dundurn Press, 1989) and Carman Miller *Painting the Map Red* (McGill-Queen's University Press, 1993). For Australia see *The Army in Australia, 1840-50* (Canberra, 1979) and, for New Zealand, those works already listed on the Maori Wars plus the very important revisionist study, James Belich *The New Zealand Wars and the Victorian Interpretation of Racial Conflict* (Auckland University Press, 1986). Another recent treatment is Tim Ryan and Bill Parham *The Colonial New Zealand Wars* (Grantham House, 1986).

African campaigns have provided much of interest, notably the Zulu War. The great classic is Donald Morris *The Washing of the Spears* (Cape, 1966) but his version of Isandlwana has been questioned and the war itself has now been covered with a wide range of modern revisionist histories. Foremost among these are the works by John Laband including *Kingdom in Crisis: The Zulu Response to the British Invasion of 1879* (Manchester University Press, 1992), *Lord Chelmsford's Zululand Campaign 1878-9* (Army Records Society, 1994) and (with Paul Thompson) *Kingdom and Colony at War* (University of Natal Press, 1990). Other modern works include Philip Gon *The Road to Isandlwana* (Donker, 1979) and A. Durning and C. Ballard (editors) *The Anglo-Zulu War: Modern Perspectives* (Cape Town, 1981). Ian Knight has written a number of popular well-illustrated studies based on the most recent scholarship including *Zulu: Isandlwana and Rorke's Drift* (Windrow and Greene, 1992), *Nothing Remains but to Fight: The Defence of Rorke's Drift, 1879* (Greenhill Books, 1993), *Brave Men's Blood* (Greenhill Books, 1990) and (with Ian Castle) *The Zulu War Then and Now* (After the Battle, 1993) and *Fearful Hard Times: The Siege and Relief of Eshowe* (Greenhill Books, 1994). On the Wolseley campaign to relieve Gordon see Julian Symons *England's Pride* (Hamish Hamilton, 1965) while the campaigns in the eastern Sudan have been covered by Brian Robson *Fuzzy Wuzzy* (Spellmount, 1993). One of a number of recent overall surveys is Henry Keown-Boyd *A Good Dusting: The Sudan Campaigns, 1883-1899* (Leo Cooper, 1986) and for the centenary of Omdurman Edward Spiers (editor) *Sudan: The Reconquest Reappraised* (Frank Cass, 1998). The Boer War of 1880-1881 is covered in Joseph Lehmann *The First Boer War* (Cape, 1972). Rather surprisingly, Abyssinia has been the subject of two books, Frederick Myatt *The March to Magdala* (Leo Cooper, 1970) and Darrell Bates *The Abyssinian Difficulty* (Oxford University Press, 1979).

The South African War has also proved popular over the years. Among many accounts are Julian Symons *Buller's Campaigns* (Hamish Hamilton, 1962) and Oliver Ransford *The Battle of Spion Kop* (Murray, 1969). For the three sieges of Mafeking, Kimberley and Ladysmith respectively, see Brian Gardner *Mafeking: A Victorian Legend* (Cassell, 1966), the same author's *The Lion's Cage* (Arthur Barker, 1969) and Kenneth Griffiths *Thank God We Kept the Flag Flying* (Hutchinson, 1974). However, by far the best books on the war are Thomas Pakenham *The Boer War* (Weidenfeld and Nicolson, 1979) and Philip Warwick (editor) *The South African War* (Longman, 1980).

Attention is also drawn to the Victorian Military Society, whose journal *Soldiers of the Queen* attains a consistently high standard.

Index